# Low Cholesterol Cookbook for Beginners

Copyright Notice

© 2025 by Tanya Norris. All rights reserved.

No part of this book may be reproduced, distributed or transmitted in any form or by any means, including photocopying, recording or other electronic or mechanical methods, without the prior written permission of the publisher, except in the case of brief quotations embodied in critical reviews and certain other non-commercial uses permitted by copyright law.

Disclaimer

This cookbook provides general information and recipes for a low cholesterol diet. It is not intended as a substitute for professional medical advice, diagnosis or treatment. Always seek the advice of your physician or other qualified health provider with any questions you may have regarding a medical condition or dietary changes.

The nutritional information provided in this cookbook is based on approximate calculations and should not be considered a guarantee. Ingredients and nutritional values may vary based on brands, preparation methods and individual dietary needs. The author and publisher make no claims to the accuracy, completeness or efficacy of the information in this book and shall not be held liable for any adverse effects or consequences arising from the use of any recipe or information contained within.

By using this cookbook, you agree to take full responsibility for any dietary or health choices you make based on the information presented here.

# TABLE OF CONTENTS

## INTRODUCTION ........................................................... 5
- Welcome ............................................................................ 5
- Understanding Cholesterol ................................................ 5
- Why Managing Cholesterol Matters ................................. 5
- The Basics of a Low Cholesterol Diet ............................... 6
- Meal Planning for Success ................................................ 7
- Cooking Techniques for Heart Health ............................... 7
- Managing Cravings Without Compromise ........................ 8
- Lifestyle Tips for Low Cholesterol Living ......................... 8
- Dining Out on a Low Cholesterol Diet .............................. 9
- Troubleshooting Common Challenges ............................ 10
- Frequently Asked Questions ........................................... 10

## HEART-SMART BREAKFASTS ..........................................
- Banana and Walnut Whole-Grain Pancakes .................. 13
- Avocado and Spinach Egg White Omelette ................... 13
- Quinoa Breakfast Bowl with Nuts and Pomegranate ... 14
- Sweet Potato and Kale Breakfast Hash ......................... 14
- Oatmeal with Almond Milk, Cinnamon and Pears ......... 15
- Zucchini and Red Pepper Breakfast Muffins (Egg-Free) 15
- Green Smoothie Bowl with Granola and Kiwi ............... 16
- Spinach and Mushroom Tofu Scramble ......................... 16
- Carrot Cake Overnight Oats ........................................... 17
- Veggie-Packed Breakfast Burrito ................................... 17
- Walnut and Date Breakfast Bars ................................... 18
- Sweet Potato Bowl with Almonds and Cinnamon ........ 18
- Lentil and Veggie Breakfast Scramble .......................... 19
- Berry and Almond Butter Breakfast Wrap .................... 19
- Veggie-Packed Savoury Oatmeal .................................. 20
- Buckwheat Pancakes with Warm Berry Compote ......... 20
- Sweet Corn and Zucchini Breakfast Fritters ................. 21
- Pumpkin and Oat Breakfast Porridge ............................ 21
- Baked Oatmeal Cups with Blueberries and Walnuts .... 22
- Quinoa Bowl with Sautéed Kale and Mushrooms ........ 22

## LOW-CHOLESTEROL BOWLS: SOUPS AND SALADS ............
- Corn and Sweet Potato Chowder (No Cream) ............. 24
- Broccoli and Cranberry Salad with Almonds ................ 24
- Lentil and Spinach Soup with a Hint of Lemon ............ 25
- Thai-Inspired Cabbage Slaw with Peanut Dressing ...... 25
- Cabbage and White Bean Soup ..................................... 26
- Zucchini Noodle Salad with Pesto .................................. 26
- Broccoli and Pea Soup with Fresh Mint ....................... 27
- Edamame and Brown Rice Salad ................................... 27
- Tomato and Barley Soup with Thyme ........................... 28
- Roasted Beet and Avocado Salad .................................. 28
- Summer Gazpacho with Fresh Herbs ............................ 29
- Herb-Roasted Potato Salad (No Mayo) ........................ 29
- Quinoa and Kale Detox Soup ......................................... 30
- Mixed Greens with Orange and Pumpkin Seeds ........... 30
- Roasted Garlic and Mushroom Soup ............................. 31
- Warm Roasted Vegetable Salad with Balsamic Glaze ... 31
- Cauliflower and Leek Soup with Garlic Croutons ...... 32
- Zesty Bean and Corn Salad ........................................... 32
- Split Pea Soup with Fresh Herbs ................................... 33
- Spinach and Strawberry Salad with Balsamic Glaze .... 33

## LOW-CHOLESTEROL MAIN DISHES ..................................
- Quinoa-Stuffed Bell Peppers with Chickpeas ............. 35
- Sweet Potato and Lentil Curry ...................................... 35
- Baked Eggplant Parmesan (Dairy-Free) ....................... 36
- Roasted Cauliflower Steaks with Chimichurri ............. 36
- Teriyaki Tofu Stir-Fry with Brown Rice ....................... 37
- Vegan Shepherd's Pie with Lentils and Sweet Potato ... 37
- Stuffed Portobello Mushrooms with Brown Rice ....... 38
- Moroccan Chickpea and Vegetable Tagine ................... 38
- Grilled Tofu Skewers with Peanut Sauce .................... 39
- Roasted Vegetable Buddha Bowl with Tahini Dressing . 39
- Cauliflower Fried Rice with Tofu .................................. 40
- Baked Cod with Lemon and Herbs ............................... 40
- Vegan Bolognese with Whole-Grain Pasta .................. 41
- Baked Salmon with Garlic, Dill and Asparagus ........... 41
- Roasted Eggplant and Chickpea Salad Bowl ............... 42
- Sweet Potato and Black Bean Enchiladas .................... 42
- Butternut Squash and Kale Risotto .............................. 43
- Hearty Vegetable and Lentil Stew ................................ 43
- Broccoli and Cashew Stir-Fry with Brown Rice ......... 44
- Mushroom and Barley Stuffed Cabbage Rolls ............. 44

## CHOLESTEROL-FRIENDLY SIDES & SNACKS .......................
- Baked Sweet Potato Wedges with Smoked Paprika ..... 46
- Baked Polenta Fries with Marinara Dip ........................ 46
- Garlic and Herb Roasted Mushrooms ........................... 47
- Baked Zucchini Sticks with Marinara Sauce ................ 47
- Smoky Eggplant Dip with Whole-Grain Crackers ........ 48
- Herb-Infused Brown Rice Pilaf ...................................... 48
- Crispy Baked Tofu Nuggets .......................................... 49
- Avocado and Lime Guacamole with Veggie Sticks ....... 49
- Spicy Roasted Chickpeas ............................................... 50
- Baked Falafel Bites with Cucumber Yogurt Sauce ...... 50
- Sesame Green Beans with Soy Glaze ........................... 51
- Broccoli Slaw with Sesame Dressing ........................... 51
- Hearty Lentil and Veggie Pâté ...................................... 52
- Smashed Baby Potatoes with Garlic and Chives ......... 52
- Cauliflower Mash with Fresh Thyme ........................... 53
- Sweet Corn Salad with Lime and Cilantro .................. 53
- Roasted Carrot and Parsnip Medley ............................. 54
- Balsamic Glazed Roasted Pearl (baby) Onions ........... 54
- Roasted Bell Pepper Hummus with Pita Wedges ........ 55
- Coconut-Lime Cauliflower Rice ..................................... 55

## CHOLESTEROL-CONSCIOUS DESSERT DELIGHTS

- Coconut Milk Rice Pudding with Mango ..... 57
- Baked Cinnamon Pears with Walnuts ..... 57
- Avocado Chocolate Mousse ..... 58
- Vegan Apple Crumble with Oats ..... 58
- Sweet Potato Brownies with Cacao ..... 59
- Chocolate-Covered Dates with Almond Butter Filling ..... 59
- Sugar-Free Lemon Coconut Bars ..... 60
- Mango and Passionfruit Sorbet ..... 60
- Vegan Blueberry Almond Tart ..... 61
- Almond and Date Energy Bars ..... 61
- Apricot and Quinoa Cookies ..... 62
- Roasted Cherry and Almond Crisp ..... 62
- Vegan Chocolate Banana Bread ..... 63
- Sesame and Coconut Mochi Bites ..... 63
- Vanilla Cashew Cream Pudding with Pomegranate ..... 64
- Vegan Orange and Almond Cake ..... 64
- Lemon and Blueberry Polenta Cake ..... 65
- Cinnamon-Spiced Roasted Almond Butter Bark ..... 65
- Vegan Espresso Almond Truffles Recipe ..... 66
- Almond Milk Panna Cotta with Raspberry Coulis ..... 66

## HEART-SMART SMOOTHIES & SIPS

- Raspberry and Mint Lemonade Smoothie ..... 68
- Blueberry Oatmeal Breakfast Smoothie ..... 68
- Tropical Pineapple and Spinach Smoothie Recipe ..... 69
- Berry Burst Chia Smoothie ..... 69
- Green Detox Smoothie with Cucumber and Kiwi ..... 69
- Carrot Ginger Immunity Smoothie ..... 70
- Zesty Lemon Kale Smoothie ..... 70
- Matcha Green Tea and Banana Smoothie ..... 71
- Orange Sunshine Smoothie with Turmeric ..... 71
- Spiced Pumpkin Pie Smoothie ..... 71
- Golden Turmeric Almond Latte ..... 72
- Iced Hibiscus and Pomegranate Tea ..... 72
- Minty Cucumber Cooler ..... 73
- Cranberry Ginger Fizz ..... 73
- Blueberry Lemon Infused Water ..... 73
- Chia-Infused Limeade ..... 74
- Zesty Grapefruit and Ginger Spritz ..... 74
- Spiced Apple Cider Mocktail ..... 75
- Beet and Berry Antioxidant Juice ..... 75
- Pear Cardamom Shake ..... 75

## 30-DAY LOW CHOLESTEROL MEAL PLAN ..... 76
## COOKING MEASUREMENTS & CONVERSIONS ..... 79
## INDEX ..... 80

# Introduction

## Welcome

We are thrilled to welcome you to the Low Cholesterol Cookbook for Beginners, your ultimate guide to heart-healthy, delicious and easy-to-make meals. This cookbook is designed to empower you with the knowledge, tools and recipes needed to take control of your cholesterol levels while enjoying flavourful and satisfying dishes.

Whether you are looking to improve your heart health, manage cholesterol levels or simply embrace a healthier way of eating, this book is here to help. Inside, you will find a variety of carefully crafted recipes that prioritize wholesome, nutrient-dense ingredients proven to lower LDL ("bad") cholesterol and support HDL ("good") cholesterol.

**What You'll Find Inside**

This cookbook offers a wide range of recipes, from energizing breakfasts and quick lunches to hearty dinners and guilt-free desserts, ensuring that every meal and craving is covered. Each recipe includes detailed nutritional information, empowering you to make informed choices about your diet and overall health. You will also find practical tips and techniques to help you shop for ingredients, plan meals and prepare dishes that are both delicious and heart healthy. Beyond the recipes, this book provides inspiration for a healthier lifestyle by including guidance on incorporating physical activity and mindfulness into your routine, complementing your dietary efforts.

We hope this cookbook inspires you to take control of your health, one meal at a time. Let's embark on your journey to a healthier heart and a more flavourful life together!

## Understanding Cholesterol

Cholesterol often carries a negative connotation, but it is essential for your body to function properly. Understanding what cholesterol is and how it works is a crucial step toward improving your heart health and overall well-being.

**What is Cholesterol?**

Cholesterol is a waxy, fat-like substance found in every cell of your body. It is vital for producing hormones, building cell membranes and aiding in the production of vitamin D and bile. While cholesterol is necessary for these processes, too much of it in your blood can cause serious health problems.

The cholesterol in your body comes from two sources: the food you eat and what your liver naturally produces. The liver generates all the cholesterol your body needs, meaning dietary intake can easily lead to an excess if not managed carefully.

**LDL, HDL and Triglycerides: The Key Players**

Cholesterol travels through your bloodstream in molecules called lipoproteins, which come in two main types: LDL and HDL.

LDL (Low-Density Lipoprotein): Often called "bad cholesterol," LDL carries cholesterol to your cells. However, when levels are too high, LDL deposits cholesterol on the walls of your arteries, forming plaque. Over time, this buildup can narrow or block arteries, leading to conditions such as heart disease or stroke.

HDL (High-Density Lipoprotein): Known as "good cholesterol," HDL works to remove excess cholesterol from your bloodstream and transport it back to your liver, where it is processed and eliminated. Higher levels of HDL are associated with a lower risk of heart disease.

Triglycerides: These are another type of fat found in your blood. When you consume more calories than your body needs, the excess is stored as triglycerides. High levels of triglycerides, especially when combined with high LDL or low HDL levels, increase the risk of cardiovascular problems.

## Why Managing Cholesterol Matters

Although cholesterol has a reputation for being harmful, it performs several essential functions. It is a key building block for cell membranes, allowing cells to maintain their structure and communicate effectively. Cholesterol is also crucial for producing hormones such as estrogen, testosterone and cortisol, which regulate various bodily functions. Additionally, it aids in synthesizing vitamin D and producing bile, which helps break down dietary fats for absorption.

However, while cholesterol is necessary, your body requires a delicate balance. High levels of LDL cholesterol contribute to the development of heart disease, the leading cause of death worldwide. Plaque buildup in the arteries can result in reduced blood flow to vital organs, causing chest pain, fatigue and, in severe cases, life-threatening complications like heart attacks or strokes.

Conversely, low levels of HDL cholesterol make it harder for your body to clear excess cholesterol, exacerbating the risk of arterial plaque. High triglyceride levels further complicate the picture, leading to conditions like pancreatitis and amplifying the risks associated with high LDL cholesterol.

The good news is that these risks are largely preventable. By adopting a heart-healthy diet and making lifestyle changes, you can manage your cholesterol levels effectively and reduce your chances of developing cardiovascular diseases.

### Your Role in Balancing Cholesterol

Managing cholesterol is a lifelong process, but small, consistent efforts can yield significant rewards. Choosing foods rich in soluble fiber, like oats, beans and fruits, helps your body eliminate cholesterol. Replacing saturated fats with unsaturated fats from sources like nuts, seeds and olive oil supports heart health. Regular physical activity boosts HDL cholesterol and lowers LDL cholesterol and triglycerides, while reducing added sugars and trans fats can further protect your heart.

By understanding cholesterol's role in your body and its impact on health, you can take control of your diet and lifestyle to achieve a healthier balance. This knowledge, paired with the recipes and tips in this cookbook, will empower you to make heart-smart choices every day.

# The Basics of a Low Cholesterol Diet

A low cholesterol diet is more than just avoiding certain foods; it is about embracing nutrient-rich, heart-friendly ingredients that naturally support your health. In this chapter, we will explore what to eat, what to limit and the essential role of fiber and plant sterols in managing cholesterol levels. By the end, you will have a clear roadmap for building meals that help lower LDL cholesterol and promote overall well-being.

### What to Eat

Certain foods are natural allies in the fight against high LDL cholesterol. These ingredients not only help reduce "bad" cholesterol but also provide nutrients to keep your heart strong and healthy.

### Foods That Lower LDL Cholesterol

**Oats and Whole Grains:** Start your day with oatmeal or include barley and whole-wheat products in your meals. These grains are rich in soluble fiber, which binds to cholesterol and helps remove it from your bloodstream.
**Fruits and Vegetables:** Apples, citrus fruits, berries and leafy greens like spinach and kale are high in fiber and antioxidants. They combat oxidative stress and reduce cholesterol levels.
**Legumes and Beans:** Lentils, chickpeas and black beans are excellent sources of soluble fiber and plant protein, making them perfect for replacing high-fat meats.
**Healthy Fats:** Unsaturated fats found in avocados, nuts, seeds and olive oil can replace saturated fats, lowering LDL cholesterol and raising HDL cholesterol.
**Fatty Fish:** Salmon, mackerel and sardines are rich in omega-3 fatty acids, which reduce triglycerides and support heart health.
**Plant Sterol-Enriched Foods:** Foods fortified with plant sterols, like certain margarine spreads, juices and cereals, actively block cholesterol absorption in the digestive system.

By incorporating these foods into your meals, you create a foundation for a diet that supports your heart while satisfying your taste buds.

### What to Limit

Just as some foods help reduce cholesterol, others can raise LDL cholesterol and contribute to cardiovascular problems. Knowing what to limit is just as important as knowing what to eat.

**High-Cholesterol Foods:** While dietary cholesterol has less impact than once thought, certain high-cholesterol foods like organ meats, shellfish and egg yolks should be consumed in moderation, especially if you have high LDL levels.
**Saturated Fats:** These fats, found in fatty cuts of meat, butter, cheese and full-fat dairy, raise LDL cholesterol. Opt for lean proteins and low-fat or plant-based dairy alternatives instead.
**Trans Fats:** Found in processed foods like baked goods, fried snacks and margarine made with partially hydrogenated oils, trans fats significantly raise LDL cholesterol and should be avoided entirely.

**Refined Sugars and Carbs:** Excessive sugar and refined carbohydrate intake can raise triglycerides, worsening your cholesterol profile. Replace sugary snacks and white bread with whole-grain options and naturally sweet fruits.

### Putting It All Together

Building a low cholesterol diet is not about deprivation – it is about making thoughtful choices that nourish your body and protect your heart. By incorporating more fiber-rich and plant sterol-enriched foods while limiting high-cholesterol and saturated fat options, you can create meals that are as delicious as they are health-promoting.

Each recipe in this cookbook has been crafted to include these heart-healthy ingredients, helping you take practical steps toward lowering LDL cholesterol and improving your overall well-being. Remember, small, consistent changes can lead to lasting improvements.

# Meal Planning for Success

Embarking on a low cholesterol diet may seem daunting at first, but thoughtful meal planning can make it both manageable and enjoyable. With the right strategies and a well-stocked kitchen, you can save time, reduce stress and stay consistent on your journey to better health.

### Building a Low Cholesterol Meal Plan

A successful low cholesterol meal plan centers around whole, nutrient-dense foods that actively lower LDL cholesterol and support heart health. Incorporate fiber-rich foods like oats, lentils, beans, fruits and vegetables, which help remove cholesterol from your body. Healthy fats such as avocados, nuts, seeds and olive oil should replace saturated fats, while lean proteins like fatty fish, plant-based options and skinless poultry provide essential nutrients. Whole grains, including brown rice, quinoa and whole-grain pasta, offer long-lasting energy and satiety. By focusing on these ingredients, you will naturally align your meals with heart-healthy goals.

### How to Save Time and Stay Consistent

Consistency starts with preparation. Dedicate a small amount of time each week to plan your meals and snacks, ensuring you have everything you need on hand. Preparing large portions of soups, roasted vegetables or whole grains in advance can save you valuable time during the week. Prepping ingredients like washing and chopping produce or cooking proteins ahead of time streamlines meal preparation on busy days.

Keeping a simple rotation of 5–10 favourite meals can simplify planning while still offering variety. For example, you might have oatmeal with berries for breakfast, a quinoa salad for lunch and roasted vegetables with grilled salmon for dinner. These simple, repeatable meals ensure you stay on track without feeling overwhelmed.

### Key Staples for a Low-Cholesterol Kitchen

Stocking your kitchen with essentials makes it easy to prepare heart-healthy meals at any time. Grains like oats, quinoa and brown rice form the base of many recipes, while proteins such as canned beans, lentils and frozen fish provide flexibility. Fresh fruits and vegetables like spinach, broccoli, apples and berries are indispensable, but frozen options are excellent for convenience.

Healthy fats, including olive oil, avocado, nuts and seeds, are essential for cooking and snacking. Keep flavour enhancers like garlic, onions, herbs and spices handy to make your dishes vibrant and satisfying. Fortified foods with plant sterols, such as certain spreads or cereals, add an extra boost to help reduce cholesterol.

### Your Plan for Success

Meal planning is a simple yet powerful tool for sustaining a low cholesterol diet. By focusing on nutrient-dense foods, preparing in advance and ensuring your kitchen is stocked with staples, you make it easy to stay consistent. Each planned meal becomes a step toward a healthier heart and a more vibrant life. With these strategies, you will find that heart-healthy eating fits seamlessly into your daily routine.

# Cooking Techniques for Heart Health

The way you prepare your food can make a significant difference in managing cholesterol and promoting overall heart health. By adopting healthy cooking methods, making smart ingredient swaps and learning to read nutrition labels effectively, you can enjoy delicious meals while taking care of your heart.

### Healthy Cooking Methods

Cooking methods that minimize the use of added fats and preserve nutrients are key to heart-healthy eating. Opt for techniques like steaming, which retains the natural flavours and nutrients in vegetables, or grilling, which brings out the natural flavours of proteins without requiring excess oils. Baking and roasting are excellent for creating rich, satisfying dishes with minimal saturated fats.

Stir-frying with a small amount of olive oil is another versatile method, allowing you to cook quickly while keeping dishes flavourful and light.

### Smart Ingredient Swaps

Simple swaps can significantly reduce unhealthy fats and cholesterol in your meals. Use olive oil or avocado oil instead of butter for cooking, as these contain heart-healthy monounsaturated fats. Replace full-fat dairy products with plant-based or low-fat options, such as almond milk or low-fat yogurt. Instead of using heavy cream in recipes, substitute with coconut milk or a blend of almond milk and cornstarch. For baked goods, mashed bananas or applesauce can replace butter while adding natural sweetness and moisture.

### Understanding Labels: Decoding Nutrition Information

Reading and understanding nutrition labels is essential for making heart-smart choices. Pay close attention to the following:
**Cholesterol**: Look for foods labelled "low cholesterol" or containing less than 20 mg of cholesterol per serving.
**Saturated Fats**: Aim for products with 1 gram or less of saturated fat per serving to limit artery-clogging fats.
**Trans Fats**: Avoid any product listing "partially hydrogenated oils" or containing trans fats, as these can raise LDL cholesterol and lower HDL cholesterol.
**Total Fat:** Check the breakdown to ensure most of the fat content comes from unsaturated fats, which are healthier for your heart.
**Serving Size:** Always compare the nutritional information to the portion you intend to eat to ensure accurate tracking.

By combining healthy cooking methods, smart substitutions and an understanding of nutrition labels, you can create meals that are not only delicious but also beneficial for your heart. These small but impactful changes will help you transform everyday meals into nourishing, cholesterol-friendly dishes. With these techniques, heart-healthy cooking becomes second nature, setting you on the path to a healthier lifestyle.

# Managing Cravings Without Compromise

Cravings for sugary or high-fat foods can be challenging when following a low cholesterol diet, but they don't have to derail your progress. With thoughtful strategies and satisfying heart-healthy alternatives, you can indulge your taste buds without compromising your health.

### Strategies to Curb Cravings

Cravings often arise from habits, emotional triggers or a lack of certain nutrients. To manage them effectively, start by staying hydrated - thirst is often mistaken for hunger. Eating balanced meals with fiber, protein and healthy fats helps keep your blood sugar stable, reducing the urge for unhealthy snacks. When sugar cravings hit, choose naturally sweet options like fresh fruit or dried fruit in moderation. Pair these with a protein source, such as a handful of nuts, to enhance satisfaction. For high-fat cravings, opt for healthier alternatives like avocado, hummus or nut butter, which provide the creamy texture and rich flavour you seek without harmful saturated or trans fats. Mindful eating can also help curb cravings. Take time to savour each bite and ask yourself whether you are truly hungry or simply craving a distraction. Often, a short walk, deep breathing or a fun activity can redirect your focus.

### Heart-Healthy Snack Ideas That Satisfy

Snacking can be both enjoyable and nourishing with the right choices. Reach for crunchy options like roasted chickpeas or air-popped popcorn lightly seasoned with nutritional yeast or cinnamon for a satisfying, cholesterol-friendly treat. Fresh vegetables with a dollop of guacamole or a side of hummus provide fiber and healthy fats to keep you full. If you are craving something sweet, try a bowl of Greek yogurt topped with fresh berries and a sprinkle of chia seeds or enjoy dark chocolate with almonds for a rich, antioxidant-packed indulgence. For savoury cravings, whole-grain crackers with avocado or a hard-boiled egg sprinkled with herbs can be both delicious and filling.

Managing cravings doesn't mean giving up your favourite flavours. By planning ahead and choosing nutrient-dense alternatives, you can satisfy your taste buds while staying aligned with your heart health goals. Cravings are a normal part of life, and with these simple strategies, you can handle them with confidence and enjoy a diet that is both nourishing and indulgent.

# Lifestyle Tips for Low Cholesterol Living

Achieving a healthier heart goes beyond the plate. While diet plays a critical role in managing cholesterol, your lifestyle choices are just as important. Incorporating regular exercise, managing stress effectively and prioritizing quality sleep can amplify the benefits of your low-cholesterol diet and support overall heart health.

### Exercise and Cholesterol

Regular physical activity is one of the most effective ways to improve cholesterol levels. Exercise helps lower LDL ("bad") cholesterol while boosting HDL ("good") cholesterol, creating a healthier balance in your bloodstream. Activities like brisk walking, cycling, swimming or strength training also help maintain a healthy weight, further reducing cholesterol and improving heart function. The key is consistency. Aim for at least 150 minutes of moderate-intensity exercise per week, which can be broken into short, manageable sessions. Whether it is a morning walk, a yoga class or dancing in your living room, staying active not only benefits your cholesterol but also enhances your mood and energy levels.

### Stress Management

Chronic stress can negatively impact cholesterol levels by triggering the release of cortisol, a hormone that encourages the production of LDL cholesterol. Stress also often leads to unhealthy habits like overeating, smoking or skipping exercise, all of which can worsen cholesterol levels. Managing stress doesn't have to be complicated. Simple practices like deep breathing, meditation or mindfulness exercises can help you stay calm and focused. Regular physical activity and hobbies you enjoy, such as gardening, painting or reading, can also alleviate stress. Taking time for yourself and maintaining a positive mindset are just as crucial for your heart health as the food you eat.

### Sleep and Cholesterol

Sleep is an often-overlooked factor in cholesterol management. Poor sleep patterns disrupt hormone regulation, increasing LDL cholesterol and reducing HDL cholesterol levels. Lack of sleep also heightens stress and impairs decision-making, making it harder to stick to healthy habits. To support heart health, prioritize seven to nine hours of quality sleep each night. Establish a calming bedtime routine, such as reading, stretching or listening to soothing music. Limiting caffeine and screen time in the evening can also improve sleep quality. When your body is well-rested, it functions more efficiently, including maintaining optimal cholesterol levels.

Low cholesterol living is about more than just diet - it's a holistic approach that includes staying active, managing stress and prioritizing rest. By incorporating these lifestyle habits, you're not just supporting your heart health but enhancing your overall well-being.

# Dining Out on a Low Cholesterol Diet

Eating out doesn't have to derail your commitment to a low cholesterol diet. With a little preparation and mindful choices, you can savour dining out or attending social events while keeping your heart health in focus. This chapter provides practical tips for navigating menus and making heart-smart decisions without sacrificing flavour or enjoyment.

### Tips for Choosing Heart-Healthy Menu Options

When dining at restaurants, start by scanning the menu for dishes that align with your dietary goals. Opt for grilled, baked, steamed or roasted options rather than fried items. Lean proteins like grilled fish, skinless poultry or plant-based proteins such as lentils or tofu are excellent choices. Ask for dressings, sauces or butter to be served on the side, as these often contain hidden saturated fats and cholesterol. Focus on whole foods, such as salads with a variety of fresh vegetables, soups made with broth instead of cream or grain-based sides like quinoa or brown rice. If the menu doesn't specify, don't hesitate to ask the server about preparation methods or request modifications to make your dish more heart-healthy. Most restaurants are happy to accommodate dietary needs.

### Navigating Social Events

Social gatherings often involve indulgent food choices, but with a bit of planning, you can enjoy yourself without compromising your goals. If possible, eat a light, heart-healthy meal or snack beforehand to avoid arriving hungry and overindulging. When serving yourself, prioritize fruits, vegetables and lean proteins, and enjoy small portions of higher-fat or sugary foods if they are available. Engage in conversation or participate in activities to shift the focus away from food. If you are contributing to the meal, bring a dish that aligns with your diet, such as a colourful salad, roasted vegetables or whole-grain crackers with hummus. This ensures you'll have a healthy option to enjoy while sharing it with others.

### A Heart-Healthy Approach to Dining Out

Dining out and social events are opportunities to enjoy great food and connect with others. By making thoughtful menu choices, planning ahead and maintaining balance, you can stick to your low cholesterol goals while savouring the experience. Remember, it's not about perfection - it's about making small, consistent choices that support your heart and overall health.

# Troubleshooting Common Challenges

Embarking on a cholesterol-lowering journey comes with its own set of challenges. From maintaining motivation to navigating setbacks or incorporating the diet into family meals, it's essential to have strategies in place to keep moving forward. This chapter addresses common hurdles and provides practical solutions to ensure long-term success.

### Staying Motivated

Motivation can ebb and flow, especially when results take time. To stay focused, remind yourself of the bigger picture - improving your heart health and overall well-being. Celebrate small victories, like preparing a new heart-healthy recipe or successfully swapping unhealthy fats for healthier alternatives. Tracking your progress, whether through cholesterol levels, energy levels or simply how you feel, can also provide a boost. Surround yourself with supportive friends and family, and don't hesitate to seek encouragement or share your goals with those who can help keep you accountable.

### Dealing with Setbacks and Plateaus

Setbacks and plateaus are normal parts of any health journey and should be viewed as opportunities to reassess rather than failures. If you slip into old eating habits, focus on your next meal rather than dwelling on the mistake. Treat setbacks as learning experiences, identifying triggers or situations that may have contributed to them. Plateaus, on the other hand, may indicate a need for small adjustments, such as incorporating more physical activity, tweaking portion sizes or varying your meals to include different heart-healthy ingredients. Be patient with yourself - progress isn't always linear, but persistence pays off.

### Incorporating the Diet into Family Meals

Adopting a low cholesterol diet doesn't mean preparing separate meals for yourself and your family. Heart-healthy eating benefits everyone, so try making small changes that the whole household can enjoy. Introduce colourful fruits and vegetables into dishes, experiment with whole grains like quinoa or brown rice and use lean proteins or plant-based alternatives in family favourites. To make the transition seamless, focus on meals that are flavourful and satisfying, such as grilled chicken with roasted vegetables or a hearty lentil stew. Involve your family in meal planning and preparation, allowing them to contribute ideas and discover new favourites. When everyone feels included, the diet becomes a shared lifestyle rather than a solitary effort.

Challenges are inevitable, but they are also opportunities to strengthen your commitment and learn what works best for you. By staying motivated, addressing setbacks with patience and involving your family in heart-healthy eating, you can overcome obstacles and continue making progress. Remember, every step you take brings you closer to a healthier heart and a more fulfilling life.

# Frequently Asked Questions

Adopting a low cholesterol diet doesn't mean giving up your favourite foods or following rigid rules. Instead, it is about making informed, balanced choices that support your heart and overall well-being. In this chapter, we address some of the most frequently asked questions to provide clarity and confidence as you embrace this lifestyle.

**Q. Can I Still Eat Eggs on a Low Cholesterol Diet?**
A. Yes, you can still enjoy eggs in moderation. While egg yolks contain dietary cholesterol, recent research shows that for most people, they have less of an impact on blood cholesterol levels than previously thought. If you're managing high LDL cholesterol, it's a good idea to limit yolks to 2–3 per week and focus on egg whites, which are cholesterol-free and high in protein. You can also explore egg substitutes for baking and cooking, such as flaxseed or chia seed gels, for variety.

**Q. Is All Fat Bad for Cholesterol?**
A. No, not all fats are bad for cholesterol. In fact, healthy fats, like those found in avocados, olive oil, nuts and seeds, are essential for lowering LDL cholesterol and raising HDL cholesterol. These unsaturated fats can replace harmful saturated fats, such as those in butter, fatty meats and full-fat dairy, which contribute to higher LDL levels. Avoid trans fats altogether, as they raise LDL and lower HDL cholesterol, making them particularly harmful to heart health. The key is balance - focus on quality over quantity when it comes to fats.

**Q. What Are the Best Plant-Based Protein Options?**
A. Plant-based proteins are excellent for heart health because they are naturally cholesterol-free and low in saturated fat. Lentils, chickpeas and black beans are versatile and packed with fiber, which helps lower LDL cholesterol. Quinoa, tofu and tempeh are complete proteins, meaning they contain all essential amino acids. Nuts, seeds and edamame are also great options for snacking or adding to meals. By incorporating these

protein sources into your diet, you'll not only lower cholesterol but also enjoy a diverse and satisfying menu.

**Q. Can I Eat Cheese or Dairy on a Low Cholesterol Diet?**
A. Yes, but it is important to choose wisely. Opt for low-fat or plant-based dairy alternatives, such as almond milk, coconut yogurt or cashew cheese. If you prefer traditional dairy, choose low-fat versions of milk, yogurt and cheese, and use them sparingly. Hard cheeses like Parmesan or aged cheddar can be used as a flavour enhancer rather than a main ingredient, helping you enjoy the taste without overloading on saturated fats.

**Q. How Can I Enjoy Desserts on a Low Cholesterol Diet?**
A. Desserts can still be part of a low cholesterol diet with a few adjustments. Use heart-healthy ingredients like oats, almond flour or applesauce in baked goods, and replace butter with olive oil or avocado. Fresh fruits, dark chocolate and chia seed puddings are naturally sweet and cholesterol-friendly options. With the recipes in this cookbook, you'll find indulgent yet heart-healthy treats to satisfy your sweet tooth.

**Q. Does a Low Cholesterol Diet Mean I Can't Eat Out?**
A. Not at all. Dining out is entirely possible with mindful choices. Look for grilled, baked or steamed dishes and ask for sauces or dressings on the side to control added fats. Opt for lean proteins, whole grains and plenty of vegetables. Many restaurants accommodate dietary needs, so don't hesitate to ask questions or request modifications to suit your preferences.

**Q. Is the Low Cholesterol Diet Suitable for the Whole Family?**
A. Absolutely. A low cholesterol diet emphasizes nutrient-dense, wholesome foods that benefit everyone. By focusing on fruits, vegetables, whole grains and lean proteins, you create meals that are not only heart-healthy but also flavourful and satisfying for all ages. Involving your family in meal planning and preparation makes it easier to adopt this lifestyle together.

**Final Thoughts**

Understanding the ins and outs of a low cholesterol diet empowers you to make informed choices that align with your health goals. By embracing heart-healthy foods, balancing fats and exploring plant-based proteins, you will find this way of eating both enjoyable and sustainable. Use this book as a resource to navigate your journey confidently, knowing that every step you take contributes to a stronger, healthier heart.

# Heart-Smart Breakfasts

# Banana and Walnut Whole-Grain Pancakes

*Prep. time: 10 min | Cook time: 15 min | Serves: 2*

Ingredients:
- ½ cup whole-grain oat flour
- ¼ cup whole-wheat flour
- 1 tsp baking powder
- ¼ tsp cinnamon
- 1 medium ripe banana, mashed (about ½ cup)
- 1 large egg white
- ½ cup unsweetened almond milk or low-fat milk
- 1 tsp vanilla extract
- 2 tbsp finely chopped walnuts
- 1 tsp olive oil (for greasing the pan)

Directions:
1. In a medium bowl, mix oat flour, whole-wheat flour, baking powder and cinnamon.
2. In a separate bowl, mash banana, then whisk in egg white, almond milk and vanilla extract until combined.
3. Gradually mix the wet ingredients into the dry ingredients until combined. Fold in chopped walnuts.
4. Heat a non-stick skillet over medium heat and lightly grease it with 1 tsp of olive oil or use a cooking spray.
5. Pour ¼ cup of batter onto the skillet for each pancake. Cook for 2–3 minutes or until bubbles form on the surface. Flip and cook for another 1–2 minutes. Repeat with the remaining batter.
6. Stack pancakes on a plate and garnish with additional banana slices or a sprinkle of walnuts, if desired.
   *For a touch of sweetness, drizzle with 1 tsp of pure maple syrup or honey.

Nutritional Information (per serving): Calories: 210kcal; Protein: 6g; Carbohydrates: 32g; Fats: 6g; Fiber: 5g; Cholesterol: 0mg; Sodium: 110mg; Potassium: 300mg

# Avocado and Spinach Egg White Omelette

*Prep. time: 10 min | Cook time: 10 min | Serves: 2*

Ingredients:
- 2 cups fresh spinach, loosely packed
- 8 large egg whites
- 1 small avocado, thinly sliced
- 6 cherry tomatoes, halved
- 1 tsp olive oil, divided
- 1 clove garlic, minced
- ¼ tsp black pepper
- ½ tsp Herbs de Provence or Italian seasoning

Directions:
1. Separate egg whites. Rinse and pat dry spinach. Thinly slice avocado and halve cherry tomatoes.
2. Heat ½ tsp olive oil in a non-stick skillet over medium heat. Add minced garlic, sauté for 30 seconds until fragrant. Add spinach and cook for 1–2 minutes until wilted. Remove from the pan and set aside.
3. In a medium bowl, whisk egg whites with black pepper and Herbs de Provence or Italian seasoning.
4. Heat the remaining ½ tsp olive oil in the same skillet over medium heat. Cook half of the egg whites for 2–3 minutes, then flip and cook for 1 more minute. Repeat with the remaining egg whites.
5. Place half of the cooked spinach, a few slices of avocado and halved cherry tomatoes on one half of each omelette. Fold the other half over to create a semi-circle and serve.

Nutritional Information (per serving): Calories: 140kcal; Protein: 12g; Carbohydrates: 6g; Fats: 7g; Fiber: 3g; Cholesterol: 0mg; Sodium: 50mg; Potassium: 450mg

# Quinoa Breakfast Bowl with Nuts and Pomegranate

*Prep. time: 10 min | Cook time: 15 min | Serves: 2*

Ingredients:
- ½ cup uncooked quinoa
- ¼ cup unsweetened almond milk
- ¼ cup pomegranate seeds
- 2 tbsp chopped almonds or walnuts
- 1 tbsp ground flaxseed
- 1 tsp honey or maple syrup (optional)
- ¼ tsp cinnamon
- ½ tsp vanilla extract
- Fresh mint leaves (for garnish)

Directions:
1. Rinse quinoa under cold water to remove any bitterness.
2. In a small saucepan, combine quinoa and 1 cup of water. Bring to a boil, then reduce heat to low, cover and simmer for 12–15 minutes until quinoa is fully cooked.
3. Stir almond milk, cinnamon and vanilla extract into the cooked quinoa. Simmer on low for 2 minutes, stirring occasionally, until creamy.
4. Divide quinoa into two bowls. Top each bowl with pomegranate seeds, chopped nuts and ground flaxseed.
5. Drizzle with honey or maple syrup, if desired, garnish with fresh mint leaves and serve.

Nutritional Information (per serving): Calories: 230kcal; Protein: 7g; Carbohydrates: 36g; Fats: 7g; Fiber: 5g; Cholesterol: 0mg; Sodium: 15mg; Potassium: 300mg

# Sweet Potato and Kale Breakfast Hash

*Prep. time: 10 min | Cook time: 20 min | Serves: 2*

Ingredients:
- 1 medium sweet potato, peeled and diced into small cubes
- 2 cups fresh kale, chopped and stems removed
- ½ small red onion, finely chopped
- ½ red bell pepper, diced
- 1 clove garlic, minced
- 1 tbsp olive oil, divided
- ½ tsp smoked paprika
- ¼ tsp black pepper
- ¼ tsp turmeric
- 1 tbsp fresh parsley, chopped (for garnish)

Directions:
1. Bring a small pot of water to a boil. Add diced sweet potato and cook for 5–7 minutes, until just tender but not mushy. Drain and set aside.
2. Heat ½ tbsp of olive oil in a large non-stick skillet over medium heat. Add onion, bell pepper and garlic. Sauté for 3–4 minutes until softened.
3. Push vegetables to one side of the skillet. Add the remaining ½ tbsp of olive oil and sweet potato cubes. Sprinkle with smoked paprika, black pepper and turmeric. Cook for 5–6 minutes, stirring occasionally, until sweet potatoes are golden.
4. Add kale to the skillet and toss with the other ingredients. Cook for 2–3 minutes, stirring, until kale is wilted.
5. Divide hash evenly between two plates. Garnish with fresh parsley, if desired and serve.

Nutritional Information (per serving): Calories: 150 kcal; Protein: 3g; Carbohydrates: 24g; Fats: 7 g; Fiber: 5g; Cholesterol: 0mg; Sodium: 40mg; Potassium: 450mg

# Oatmeal with Almond Milk, Cinnamon and Pears

*Prep. time: 5 min | Cook time: 10 min | Serves: 2*

Ingredients:
- 1 cup rolled oats
- 2 cups unsweetened almond milk
- 1 medium pear, diced (reserve a few slices for garnish)
- ½ tsp cinnamon
- ½ tsp vanilla extract
- 1 tbsp ground flaxseed
- 1 tbsp chopped walnuts
- 1 tsp maple syrup or honey (optional)
- A pinch of nutmeg

Directions:
1. In a medium saucepan, combine rolled oats and almond milk. Cook over medium heat, stirring occasionally, for 5–7 minutes or until oats are tender and creamy.
2. Stir in diced pear, cinnamon, vanilla extract and nutmeg. Cook for another 2–3 minutes, stirring occasionally.
3. Remove oatmeal from heat and stir in ground flaxseed.
4. Divide oatmeal evenly between two bowls. Top each bowl with reserved pear slices, a sprinkle of chopped walnuts and a drizzle of maple syrup or honey, if desired.

    *Pair with a cup of green tea or herbal tea for added antioxidants.

Nutritional Information (per serving): Calories: 210 kcal; Protein: 6 g; Carbohydrates: 38 g; Fats: 5 g; Fiber: 6 g; Cholesterol: 0 mg; Sodium: 30 mg; Potassium: 320 mg

# Zucchini and Red Pepper Breakfast Muffins (Egg-Free)

*Prep. time: 10 min | Cook time: 25 min | Serves: 2 (Makes 4 muffins)*

Ingredients:
- ½ cup whole-grain flour
- ¼ cup rolled oats
- ½ tsp baking powder
- ¼ tsp baking soda
- ¼ tsp smoked paprika
- ¼ tsp black pepper
- ½ cup grated zucchini (squeeze excess moisture)
- ¼ cup finely diced red bell pepper
- ¼ cup unsweetened almond milk
- 2 tbsp ground flaxseed + 6 tbsp water (flax egg replacement)
- 1 tsp olive oil

Directions:
1. Preheat oven to 180°C (350°F). Line a muffin tin with 4 paper liners or grease lightly with olive oil.
2. In a small bowl, mix ground flaxseed with water and let sit for 5 minutes until it thickens.
3. In a medium bowl, combine flour, rolled oats, baking powder, baking soda, paprika and black pepper.
4. In a medium bowl, mix grated zucchini, diced red pepper, almond milk, olive oil and flax egg, until combined.
5. Gradually fold the wet ingredients into the dry ingredients, stirring until just combined. Avoid overmixing.
6. Divide batter evenly among the 4 prepared muffin cups. Bake in the preheated oven for 20–25 minutes or until a toothpick inserted into the center of a muffin comes out clean.
7. Cool muffins in the tin for 5 minutes before transferring to a wire rack. Serve warm or at room temperature.

Nutritional Information (per serving): Calories: 140 kcal; Protein: 4 g; Carbohydrates: 18 g; Fats: 5 g; Fiber: 3 g; Cholesterol: 0 mg; Sodium: 120 mg; Potassium: 250 mg

# Green Smoothie Bowl with Granola and Kiwi

*Prep. time: 10 min | Cook time: 0 min | Serves: 2*

Ingredients:
- 1 medium ripe banana, frozen
- 1 cup fresh spinach, loosely packed
- ½ cup unsweetened almond milk
- ½ cup frozen mango chunks
- 1 tbsp ground flaxseed
- 1 tsp honey or maple syrup (optional)
- 1 kiwi, peeled and sliced
- ¼ cup low-sugar granola
- 1 tbsp chia seeds
- Fresh mint leaves (for garnish)

Directions:
1. In a blender, combine frozen banana, spinach, almond milk, mango chunks, flaxseed and honey, if using. Blend until smooth and creamy. Adjust consistency by adding more almond milk, if needed.
2. Divide smoothie base evenly between two bowls.
3. Arrange kiwi slices, granola and chia seeds on top of each bowl.
4. Garnish with fresh mint leaves and serve.

Nutritional Information (per serving): Calories: 190 kcal; Protein: 4 g; Carbohydrates: 35 g; Fats: 4 g; Fiber: 6 g; Cholesterol: 0 mg; Sodium: 40 mg; Potassium: 450 mg

# Spinach and Mushroom Tofu Scramble

*Prep. time: 10 min | Cook time: 0 min | Serves: 2*

Ingredients:
- 1 block (225gm/8oz) firm tofu, crumbled
- 1 cup fresh spinach, chopped
- ½ cup mushrooms, sliced
- ¼ small red onion, finely chopped
- 1 clove garlic, minced
- ¼ tsp turmeric
- ½ tsp smoked paprika
- ¼ tsp black pepper
- 1 tbsp nutritional yeast
- ½ tsp olive oil
- 1 tbsp fresh parsley, chopped (for garnish)

Directions:
1. Press tofu to remove excess water. Crumble it into small, scramble-like pieces using your hands or a fork. Wash and chop spinach, slice mushrooms and finely chop onion and garlic.
2. Heat olive oil in a non-stick skillet over medium heat. Add onion and garlic, sautéing for 2 minutes until fragrant. Add mushrooms and cook for 3 minutes until softened.
3. Push vegetables to one side of the skillet and add crumbled tofu. Sprinkle turmeric, smoked paprika, black pepper and nutritional yeast over the tofu. Stir well to combine. Cook for 3–4 minutes, stirring occasionally, until tofu is heated through and lightly golden.
4. Stir spinach into the tofu mixture. Cook for 1–2 minutes until spinach is wilted.
5. Divide scramble between two plates. Garnish with fresh parsley and serve.

Nutritional Information (per serving): Calories: 210 kcal; Protein: 6 g; Carbohydrates: 28 g; Fats: 8 g; Fiber: 5 g; Cholesterol: 0 mg; Sodium: 120 mg; Potassium: 250 mg

# Carrot Cake Overnight Oats

*Prep. time: 10 min | Setting Time: 4-8 hours (overnight) | Serves: 2*

Ingredients:
- 1 cup rolled oats
- 1 cup unsweetened almond milk
- ½ cup grated carrot
- ¼ cup raisins
- 1 tbsp ground flaxseed
- ½ tsp cinnamon
- ¼ tsp nutmeg
- ½ tsp vanilla extract
- 1 tbsp maple syrup (optional)
- 1 tbsp chopped walnuts (for garnish)
- 2 tbsp unsweetened coconut flakes (for garnish)

Directions:
1. In a medium mixing bowl, combine rolled oats, almond milk, grated carrot, raisins, ground flaxseed, cinnamon, nutmeg, vanilla extract and maple syrup. Stir well to ensure all ingredients are evenly mixed.
2. Divide mixture evenly into two jars or bowls with lids. Cover and refrigerate for at least 4 hours or overnight.
3. Before serving, give oats a good stir. Top each serving with chopped walnuts and coconut flakes.
4. Serve cold or warm it up in the microwave for 1–2 minutes, if preferred and serve.

Nutritional Information (per serving): Calories: 220 kcal; Protein: 6 g; Carbohydrates: 38 g; Fats: 6 g; Fiber: 6 g; Cholesterol: 0 mg; Sodium: 50 mg; Potassium: 350 mg

# Veggie-Packed Breakfast Burrito

*Prep. time: 10 min | Cook time: 10 min | Serves: 2*

Ingredients:
- 2 8-inch whole-grain tortillas
- 1 cup fresh spinach, chopped
- ½ cup cooked black beans, rinsed and drained
- ½ cup bell peppers (any colour), diced
- ½ cup zucchini, diced
- ¼ cup sweetcorn kernels, cooked
- 1 clove garlic, minced
- ¼ tsp smoked paprika
- ¼ tsp ground cumin
- 1 tsp olive oil
- ½ avocado, diced (for filling or garnish)

Directions:
1. Heat 1 tsp of olive oil in a non-stick skillet over medium heat. Add garlic and bell peppers, sautéing for 2–3 minutes until softened.
2. Stir in zucchini, spinach, sweetcorn, smoked paprika and cumin. Cook for another 2–3 minutes until zucchini is tender and spinach is wilted. Add black beans and cook for 1–2 more minutes to heat through.
3. Warm tortillas in a dry skillet or microwave for 10–15 seconds to make them pliable.
4. Divide veggie filling evenly between two tortillas, placing it in the center. Top each with sliced avocado.
5. Fold in the sides of each tortilla, then roll tightly from the bottom to create a burrito.
6. Slice burritos in half and enjoy warm. Pair with a small side of mixed green salad for a complete breakfast.

Nutritional Information (per serving): Calories: 260 kcal; Protein: 9 g; Carbohydrates: 36 g; Fats: 8 g; Fiber: 9 g; Cholesterol: 0 mg; Sodium: 140 mg; Potassium: 530 mg

# Walnut and Date Breakfast Bars

*Prep. time: 10 min | Cook time: 20 min | Serves: 2*

Ingredients:
- ½ cup rolled oats
- ¼ cup walnuts, finely chopped
- ¼ cup dates, pitted and finely chopped
- 2 tbsp ground flaxseed
- 2 tbsp unsweetened almond butter
- 2 tbsp maple syrup or honey (optional)
- ½ tsp vanilla extract
- ¼ tsp cinnamon
- Pinch of salt

Directions:
1. Preheat your oven to 180°C (350°F)
   Line a small baking dish or loaf tin with parchment paper.
2. In a medium mixing bowl, combine rolled oats, walnuts, dates, flaxseed, cinnamon and a pinch of salt.
3. In a small saucepan over low heat, mix almond butter, maple syrup and vanilla extract until smooth and warmed through, about 1–2 minutes.
4. Pour almond butter mixture into the dry ingredients and stir until well combined.
5. Press mixture firmly into the baking dish and bake for 15–20 minutes until edges are golden brown.
6. Allow mixture to cool completely in the dish, about 15 minutes. Once cooled, remove from the dish and cut into 4 small bars and serve.
   *Bars can also be wrapped and stored in the fridge for up to 5 days.

Nutritional Information (per serving): Calories: 190 kcal; Protein: 4 g; Carbohydrates: 24 g; Fats: 8 g; Fiber: 4 g; Cholesterol: 0 mg; Sodium: 20 mg; Potassium: 220 mg

# Sweet Potato Bowl with Almonds and Cinnamon

*Prep. time: 5 min | Cook time: 20 min | Serves: 2*

Ingredients:
- 1 medium sweet potato, peeled and diced
- ¼ cup unsweetened almond milk
- ½ tsp cinnamon
- 1 tsp vanilla extract
- 1 tbsp maple syrup (optional)
- 2 tbsp chopped almonds (for garnish)
- 1 tbsp ground flaxseed (for garnish)
- ¼ cup fresh berries (for garnish)

Directions:
1. Bring a pot of water to a boil and add diced sweet potato.
   Cook for 10–12 minutes or until tender. Drain and let cool slightly.
2. Transfer cooked sweet potato to a bowl and mash with a fork or potato masher until smooth. Stir in almond milk, cinnamon vanilla extract and maple syrup, if using. Mix until creamy and well combined.
3. Toast chopped almonds in a dry skillet over medium heat for 1–2 minutes, until golden and fragrant.
4. Divide mashed sweet potato mixture evenly between two bowls. Top each bowl with toasted almonds, ground flaxseed and fresh berries and serve immediately.

Nutritional Information (per serving): Calories: 210 kcal; Protein: 4 g; Carbohydrates: 32 g; Fats: 7 g; Fiber: 6 g; Cholesterol: 0 mg; Sodium: 20 mg; Potassium: 400 mg

# Lentil and Veggie Breakfast Scramble

*Prep. time: 10 min | Cook time: 10 min | Serves: 2*

Ingredients:
- ½ cup green or brown lentils, cooked
- ½ cup zucchini, diced
- ½ cup bell peppers (any color), diced
- ¼ cup red onion, finely chopped
- 1 clove garlic, minced
- 1 cup fresh spinach, chopped
- ¼ tsp ground turmeric
- ¼ tsp black pepper
- 1 tsp olive oil
- 1 tbsp fresh parsley or coriander, chopped (for garnish)

Directions:
1. If using dried lentils, rinse and cook them until tender, about 15–20 minutes, then drain. If using canned lentils, rinse thoroughly to remove excess sodium.
2. Heat 1 tsp of olive oil in a non-stick skillet over medium heat. Add onion and garlic, sautéing for 2 minutes until fragrant. Stir in bell peppers and zucchini, cooking for 3–4 minutes until softened.
3. Add cooked lentils to the skillet, stirring to combine with the vegetables. Toss in chopped spinach and cook for 1–2 minutes until wilted.
4. Sprinkle turmeric and black pepper over the mixture. Stir well to evenly coat all ingredients. Adjust seasoning to taste.
5. Divide scramble evenly between two plates. Garnish with fresh parsley or coriander and serve.

Nutritional Information (per serving): Calories: 190 kcal; Protein: 9 g; Carbohydrates: 23 g; Fats: 5 g; Fiber: 8 g; Cholesterol: 0 mg; Sodium: 50 mg; Potassium: 450 mg

# Berry and Almond Butter Breakfast Wrap

*Prep. time: 5 min | Cook time: 0 min | Serves: 2*

Ingredients:
- 2 8-inch whole-grain tortillas
- 2 tbsp unsweetened almond butter
- ½ cup mixed berries
- 1 tbsp ground flaxseed
- 1 tbsp chia seeds
- 1 tsp honey or maple syrup (optional)
- ¼ tsp cinnamon

Directions:
1. Wash and pat dry mixed berries. Slice strawberries, if using. Warm whole-grain tortillas in a skillet to make them more pliable.
2. Spread 1 tbsp of almond butter evenly across the center of each tortilla.
3. Scatter ¼ cup of mixed berries onto each tortilla over the almond butter. Sprinkle ground flaxseed and chia seeds evenly over the berries for a boost of heart-healthy omega-3s and fiber.
4. Drizzle with honey or maple syrup, if desired, and sprinkle with a pinch of cinnamon for added flavour.
5. Fold in the sides of the tortilla, then roll tightly into a wrap. Optionally, toast wrap lightly in a dry skillet for 1–2 minutes on each side to warm the ingredients and add a slight crispness. Slice in half and serve.

Nutritional Information (per serving): Calories: 180 kcal; Protein: 15 g; Carbohydrates: 8 g; Fats: 7 g; Fiber: 3 g; Cholesterol: 0 mg; Sodium: 120 mg; Potassium: 450 mg.

# Veggie-Packed Savoury Oatmeal

*Prep. time: 5 min | Cook time: 10 min | Serves: 2*

Ingredients:
- 1 cup rolled oats
- 2 cups low-sodium vegetable broth
- ½ cup zucchini, diced
- ½ cup bell peppers (any color), diced
- 1 tsp olive oil
- ¼ cup red onion, finely chopped
- 1 clove garlic, minced
- ½ tsp smoked paprika
- 1 tbsp fresh parsley or chives, chopped (for garnish)

Directions:
1. In a medium saucepan, bring vegetable broth to a boil. Stir in oats, reduce heat to medium and simmer for 5–7 minutes, stirring occasionally, until creamy.
2. While oats are cooking, heat olive oil in a non-stick skillet over medium heat. Add garlic and red onion, sautéing for 1–2 minutes until fragrant. Add zucchini and bell peppers, cooking for 3–4 minutes until tender.
3. Stir sautéed vegetables into the cooked oats. Add smoked paprika, stirring to combine.
4. Divide savoury oatmeal evenly between two bowls. Garnish with fresh parsley or chives and serve.

Nutritional Information (per serving): Calories: 190 kcal; Protein: 6 g; Carbohydrates: 30 g; Fats: 4 g; Fiber: 5 g; Cholesterol: 0 mg; Sodium: 150 mg; Potassium: 350 mg

# Buckwheat Pancakes with Warm Berry Compote

*Prep. time: 10 min | Cook time: 15 min | Serves: 2 (makes 6 small pancakes)*

Ingredients:
- ½ cup buckwheat flour
- ¼ cup unsweetened almond milk
- ¼ cup sparkling water
- 1 tbsp ground flaxseed + 2 tbsp water (flax egg replacement)
- 1 tsp baking powder
- ¼ tsp cinnamon
- 2 tsp maple syrup, divided (optional)
- 1 tsp olive oil
- ½ cup mixed berries (blueberries, raspberries, strawberries)
- ½ tsp lemon juice

Directions:
1. Mix ground flaxseed with water in a small bowl. Let sit for 5 minutes until thickened.
2. In a medium bowl, whisk together buckwheat flour, baking powder and cinnamon.
3. In another bowl, combine almond milk, sparkling water, flax egg and 1 tsp of maple syrup, if using.
4. Gradually add the wet ingredients to the dry ingredients, stirring until smooth. Let batter rest for 5 minutes.
5. Heat a non-stick skillet over medium heat and lightly grease with olive oil. Pour 2 tbsp of batter per pancake onto the skillet. Cook for 1–2 minutes per each side. Repeat with remaining batter.
6. In a small saucepan over medium heat, combine mixed berries, 1 tsp of maple syrup, lemon juice and 1 tbsp of water.
7. Cook for 3–5 minutes, stirring occasionally, until berries break down and form a thick, warm compote.
8. Divide pancakes between two plates. Top with berry compote, garnish with fresh mint leaves and serve.

Nutritional Information (per serving): Calories: 220 kcal; Protein: 5 g; Carbohydrates: 36 g; Fats: 5 g; Fiber: 7 g; Cholesterol: 0 mg; Sodium: 110 mg; Potassium: 250 mg

# Sweet Corn and Zucchini Breakfast Fritters

*Prep. time: 10 min | Cook time: 15 min | Serves: 2 (makes 6 fritters)*

Ingredients:
- ½ cup sweetcorn kernels, cooked
- ½ cup grated zucchini (squeeze out excess moisture)
- ¼ cup whole-grain flour
- 1 tbsp ground flaxseed + 2 tbsp water (flax egg replacement)
- 1 tbsp fresh parsley or chives, chopped
- ¼ tsp smoked paprika
- ¼ tsp garlic powder
- ¼ tsp black pepper
- ½ tsp baking powder
- 1 tsp olive oil

Directions:
1. Mix ground flaxseed with water in a small bowl. Let sit for 5 minutes until it thickens.
2. In a medium bowl, combine sweetcorn, grated zucchini, whole-grain flour, parsley or chives, smoked paprika, garlic powder, black pepper and baking powder.
3. Stir in prepared flax egg until well combined. The batter should hold together but remain slightly moist.
4. Heat a non-stick skillet over medium heat and lightly grease with olive oil.
5. Scoop 2 tbsp of the batter for each fritter onto the skillet, flattening slightly with the back of a spoon.
6. Cook for 2–3 minutes per side or until golden brown and crisp. Repeat with the remaining batter.
7. Place fritters on a plate and garnish with additional parsley or chives, if desired and serve.

Nutritional Information (per serving): Calories: 190 kcal; Protein: 6 g; Carbohydrates: 25 g; Fats: 6 g; Fiber: 4 g; Cholesterol: 0 mg; Sodium: 120 mg; Potassium: 280 mg

# Pumpkin and Oat Breakfast Porridge

*Prep. time: 10 min | Cook time: 15 min | Serves: 2*

Ingredients:
- 1 cup rolled oats
- 2 cups unsweetened almond milk
- ½ cup unsweetened pumpkin puree
- ½ tsp cinnamon
- ¼ tsp nutmeg
- ¼ tsp ground ginger
- 1 tbsp maple syrup (optional)
- 2 tbsp chopped walnuts
- 1 tbsp pumpkin seeds
- 1 tbsp ground flaxseed

Directions:
1. In a medium saucepan, combine rolled oats and almond milk. Bring to a gentle boil over medium heat, then reduce heat to low and simmer for 5 minutes, stirring occasionally.
2. Stir in pumpkin puree, cinnamon, nutmeg and ground ginger. Continue cooking for 3–5 minutes, stirring frequently, until porridge thickens and is creamy.
3. Stir in maple syrup, if desired, and adjust consistency by adding more almond milk, if needed.
4. Divide porridge between two bowls. Top with chopped walnuts, pumpkin seeds and ground flaxseed, and serve.

Nutritional Information (per serving): Calories: 210 kcal; Protein: 6 g; Carbohydrates: 32 g; Fats: 7 g; Fiber: 6 g; Cholesterol: 0 mg; Sodium: 90 mg; Potassium: 350 mg

# Baked Oatmeal Cups with Blueberries and Walnuts

*Prep. time: 10 min | Cook time: 25 min | Serves: 2 (makes 4 oatmeal cups)*

Ingredients:
- 1 cup rolled oats
- ½ cup unsweetened almond milk
- ¼ cup fresh blueberries
- 2 tbsp chopped walnuts
- 1 tbsp ground flaxseed + 2 tbsp water (flax egg replacement)
- 1 tbsp maple syrup (optional)
- ½ tsp cinnamon
- ¼ tsp baking powder
- ¼ tsp vanilla extract
- Pinch of salt

Directions:
1. Preheat oven to 180°C (350°F). Grease a muffin tin lightly with olive oil or line with paper liners.
2. In a small bowl, mix ground flaxseed with water and let it sit for 5 minutes to thicken.
3. In a medium bowl, combine rolled oats, cinnamon, baking powder and a pinch of salt.
4. In another bowl, mix almond milk, maple syrup, vanilla extract and prepared flax egg.
5. Gradually stir wet ingredients into the dry until fully combined, then gently fold in blueberries and walnuts.
6. Divide batter evenly into 4 muffin cups, filling each about ¾ full. Bake in the preheated oven for 20–25 minutes or until tops are golden brown and a toothpick inserted into the center comes out clean.
7. Let oatmeal cups cool in the tin for 5 minutes before transferring to a wire rack. Serve warm.

Nutritional Information (per serving): Calories: 190 kcal; Protein: 5 g; Carbohydrates: 28 g; Fats: 6 g; Fiber: 4 g; Cholesterol: 0 mg; Sodium: 60 mg; Potassium: 180 mg

# Quinoa Bowl with Sautéed Kale and Mushrooms

*Prep. time: 10 min | Cook time: 20 min | Serves: 2*

Ingredients:
- ½ cup quinoa, rinsed
- 1 cup water or low-sodium vegetable broth
- 2 cups fresh kale, chopped and stems removed
- 1 cup mushrooms, sliced
- 1 tsp olive oil
- 1 clove garlic, minced
- ¼ tsp smoked paprika
- ¼ tsp black pepper
- 1 tbsp fresh parsley or chives, chopped (for garnish)
- 1 tbsp nutritional yeast

Directions:
1. In a medium saucepan, combine quinoa and water or broth. Bring to a boil, then reduce heat to low, cover and simmer for 15 minutes or until quinoa is tender and liquid is absorbed. Fluff with a fork and set aside.
2. Heat 1 tsp of olive oil in a large skillet over medium heat. Add garlic and sauté for 30 seconds until fragrant.
3. Add mushrooms and cook for 4–5 minutes until golden and tender. Add kale and cook for 2–3 minutes, stirring, until wilted. Sprinkle with smoked paprika and black pepper.
4. Divide cooked quinoa between two bowls. Top each bowl with sautéed kale and mushrooms.
5. Sprinkle each bowl with nutritional yeast, garnish with fresh parsley or chives and serve.

Nutritional Information (per serving): Calories: 230 kcal; Protein: 7 g; Carbohydrates: 25 g; Fats: 9 g; Fiber: 5 g; Cholesterol: 0 mg; Sodium: 75 mg; Potassium: 450 mg

# Low-Cholesterol Bowls: Soups and Salads

# Corn and Sweet Potato Chowder (No Cream)

*Prep. time: 10 min | Cook Time: 25 mi | Serves: 2*

Ingredients:
- 1 cup sweet potato, peeled and diced
- 2 cups low-sodium vegetable broth
- ½ tsp smoked paprika
- ¼ tsp black pepper
- 1 cup fresh or frozen corn kernels
- ½ cup unsweetened almond milk
- ¼ cup onion, finely chopped
- ¼ cup celery, diced
- 1 clove garlic, minced
- 1 tsp olive oil
- 1 tbsp fresh parsley, chopped (for garnish)

Directions:
1. Heat olive oil in a pot over medium heat. Add onion, celery and garlic. Sauté for 3–4 minutes until softened.
2. Add diced sweet potato, vegetable broth, smoked paprika and black pepper to the pot. Bring to a boil, then reduce heat to low and simmer for 15 minutes or until sweet potato is tender.
3. Stir in corn kernels and almond milk. Simmer for an additional 5–7 minutes until heated through.
4. For a creamier texture, use an immersion blender to partially blend the soup, leaving some chunks for texture. Alternatively, blend half of the soup and return it to the pot.
5. Taste and adjust seasoning as needed. Divide chowder between two bowls, garnish with parsley and serve.

Nutritional Information (per serving): Calories: 180 kcal; Protein: 4 g; Carbohydrates: 34 g; Fats: 3 g; Fiber: 5 g; Cholesterol: 0 mg; Sodium: 90 mg; Potassium: 600 mg

# Broccoli and Cranberry Salad with Almonds

*Prep. time: 10 min | Cook time: 0 min | Serves: 2*

Ingredients:
- 2 cups fresh broccoli florets, chopped into bite-sized pieces
- ¼ cup dried cranberries
- ¼ cup red onion, thinly sliced
- 2 tbsp sliced almonds, toasted
- 2 tbsp fresh parsley, chopped
- 2 tbsp olive oil
- 1 tbsp apple cider vinegar
- 1 tbsp fresh lemon juice
- ½ tsp Dijon mustard
- ¼ tsp black pepper
- Pinch of salt

Directions:
1. In a large mixing bowl, combine broccoli florets, dried cranberries, red onion, sliced almonds and parsley.
2. In a small bowl, whisk together olive oil, apple cider vinegar, lemon juice, Dijon mustard, black pepper and a pinch of salt.
3. Pour dressing over the salad and toss gently to combine, ensuring all ingredients are evenly coated.
4. Divide salad into two bowls. Serve immediately or refrigerate for 10–15 minutes to allow flavours to meld.

Nutritional Information (per serving): Calories: 210 kcal; Protein: 5 g; Carbohydrates: 16 g; Fats: 14 g; Fiber: 4 g; Cholesterol: 0 mg; Sodium: 50 mg; Potassium: 350 mg

# Lentil and Spinach Soup with a Hint of Lemon

*Prep. time: 10 min | Cook time: 25 min | Serves: 2*

Ingredients:
- ½ cup dried green or brown lentils
- 2 cups low-sodium vegetable broth
- 1 cup fresh spinach, roughly chopped
- 1 medium carrot, diced
- ½ cup onion, finely chopped
- 1 clove garlic, minced
- 1 tbsp olive oil
- ¼ tsp cumin
- ¼ tsp black pepper
- 1 tbsp fresh lemon juice
- 1 tbsp fresh parsley, chopped (for garnish)

Directions:
1. In a medium pot, heat olive oil over medium heat. Add onion and garlic, sautéing for 2–3 minutes until softened and fragrant.
2. Stir in diced carrot, cumin and black pepper. Cook for 2 minutes to enhance the flavours.
3. Add lentils, vegetable broth and 1 cup of water to the pot. Bring to a boil, then reduce heat to low. Cover and simmer for 20 minutes or until lentils are tender.
4. Stir in chopped spinach and cook for an additional 2–3 minutes until wilted.
5. Remove soup from the heat and stir in fresh lemon juice. Ladle soup into bowls and garnish with parsley.

Nutritional Information (per serving): Calories: 210 kcal; Protein: 10 g; Carbohydrates: 28 g; Fats: 5 g; Fiber: 9 g; Cholesterol: 0 mg; Sodium: 120 mg; Potassium: 450 mg

# Thai-Inspired Cabbage Slaw with Peanut Dressing

*Prep. time: 15 min | Cook time: 0 min | Serves: 2*

Ingredients:
- 2 cups red cabbage, thinly sliced
- 1 cup green cabbage, thinly sliced
- ½ cup carrots, julienned or grated
- ¼ cup red bell pepper, thinly sliced
- 2 tbsp fresh coriander, chopped
- 2 tbsp unsweetened peanut butter
- 1 tbsp low-sodium soy sauce
- 1 tbsp lime juice
- 1 tsp fresh ginger, grated
- 1 clove garlic, minced
- 1 tbsp sesame seeds (for garnish)

Directions:
1. In a large mixing bowl, combine red cabbage, green cabbage, carrots, red bell pepper and fresh coriander.
2. In a small bowl, whisk together peanut butter, soy sauce, lime juice, grated ginger and minced garlic. Add water, 1 tbsp at a time, if needed, to achieve a smooth and pourable consistency.
3. Pour peanut dressing over the slaw. Toss well to ensure all vegetables are evenly coated.
4. Divide slaw between two bowls or plates. Garnish with sesame seeds and serve.

Nutritional Information (per serving): Calories: Calories: 180 kcal; Protein: 6 g; Carbohydrates: 18 g; Fats: 10 g; Fiber: 5 g; Cholesterol: 0 mg; Sodium: 180 mg; Potassium: 400 mg

# Cabbage and White Bean Soup
*Prep. time: 10 min | Cook time: 25 min | Serves: 2*

Ingredients:
- 2 cups green cabbage, shredded
- 2 cups low-sodium vegetable broth
- 1 cup cooked white beans, cannellini or navy beans
- ½ cup carrots, diced
- ½ cup celery, diced
- 2 cloves garlic, minced
- ½ cup onion, finely chopped
- 1 tbsp olive oil
- ¼ tsp smoked paprika
- 1 tsp lemon juice

Directions:
1. Heat olive oil in a medium pot over medium heat. Add onion, garlic, carrots and celery. Sauté for 5 minutes until softened.
2. Stir in shredded cabbage and smoked paprika. Cook for 2 minutes until cabbage begins to soften.
3. Pour in vegetable broth and 1 cup of water. Bring to a boil, then reduce heat to low. Cover and simmer for 15 minutes.
4. Stir in cooked white beans and simmer for an additional 5 minutes to heat through.
5. Remove soup from the heat and stir in lemon juice. Ladle soup into bowls and enjoy warm.

Nutritional Information (per serving): Calories: 180 kcal; Protein: 7 g; Carbohydrates: 22 g; Fats: 5 g; Fiber: 6 g; Cholesterol: 0 mg; Sodium: 80 mg; Potassium: 400 mg

# Zucchini Noodle Salad with Pesto
*Prep. time: 15 min | Cook time: 0 min | Serves: 2*

Ingredients:
- 2 medium zucchinis, spiralized into noodles
- ½ cup cherry tomatoes, halved
- 1 cup fresh basil leaves
- 2 tbsp olive oil
- 1 tbsp lemon juice
- 1 clove garlic
- 2 tbsp nutritional yeast
- 1 tbsp walnuts or almonds
- ¼ tsp black pepper
- 2 tbsp sunflower seeds
- 1 tbsp fresh parsley, chopped (for garnish)

Directions:
1. Use a spiralizer to turn zucchinis into noodles. Pat them dry with a paper towel to remove excess moisture.
2. In a food processor or blender, combine basil, olive oil, lemon juice, garlic, nutritional yeast, walnuts or almonds and black pepper. Blend until smooth, adding water 1 tbsp at a time to achieve desired consistency.
3. In a large mixing bowl, toss zucchini noodles with pesto until evenly coated.
4. Add cherry tomatoes and sunflower seeds, gently mixing them into the salad.
5. Divide salad between two plates or bowls. Garnish with fresh parsley and serve.

Nutritional Information (per serving): Calories: 180 kcal; Protein: 5 g; Carbohydrates: 9 g; Fats: 14 g; Fiber: 4 g; Cholesterol: 0 mg; Sodium: 45 mg; Potassium: 450 mg

# Broccoli and Pea Soup with Fresh Mint

*Prep. time: 10 min | Cook time: 20 min | Serves: 2*

Ingredients:
- 2 cups fresh broccoli florets
- 1 cup frozen or fresh peas
- 2 cups low-sodium vegetable broth
- ¼ cup onion, finely chopped
- 1 clove garlic, minced
- 1 tbsp olive oil
- ¼ tsp smoked paprika
- 1 tbsp fresh mint leaves, chopped
- 1 tsp lemon juice
- ¼ tsp black pepper

Directions:
1. Heat olive oil in a medium pot over medium heat. Add onion and garlic, and sauté for 2–3 minutes.
2. Stir in broccoli, peas and vegetable broth. Add smoked paprika for a slightly smoky depth. Bring to a boil, then reduce heat to low. Cover and simmer for 15 minutes until vegetables are tender.
3. Remove pot from the heat and let cool slightly. Using an immersion blender, blend until smooth and creamy.
4. Stir in chopped mint leaves and lemon juice. Season with black pepper to taste.
5. Ladle soup into two serving bowls, garnish with additional mint leaves and serve.

Nutritional Information (per serving): Calories: 170 kcal; Protein: 6 g; Carbohydrates: 18 g; Fats: 7 g; Fiber: 5 g; Cholesterol: 0 mg; Sodium: 95 mg; Potassium: 420 mg

# Edamame and Brown Rice Salad

*Prep. time: 10 min | Cook time: 25 min | Serves: 2*

Ingredients:
- ½ cup brown rice, uncooked
- 1 cup shelled edamame, cooked
- ½ cup red bell pepper, diced
- ¼ cup carrot, shredded
- 2 tbsp spring onion, chopped
- 2 tbsp fresh coriander or parsley, chopped
- 1 tbsp olive oil
- 1 tbsp low-sodium soy sauce
- 1 tbsp rice vinegar
- 1 tsp fresh ginger, grated
- ½ tsp maple syrup
- 1 tbsp sesame seeds (for garnish)

Directions:
1. Cook brown rice as per package instructions and let cool slightly. Boil edamame, if frozen, for 3–5 minutes, then drain and cool. Dice red bell pepper, shred carrot and chop spring onion.
2. In a small bowl, whisk olive oil, soy sauce, rice vinegar, grated ginger and maple syrup until well combined.
3. In a large mixing bowl, combine cooked brown rice, edamame, red bell pepper, carrot, spring onion and coriander or parsley. Pour dressing over the salad and toss well to coat all ingredients evenly.
4. Divide salad into two bowls. Garnish with sesame seeds for added texture and flavour and serve.

Nutritional Information (per serving): Calories: 250 kcal; Protein: 10 g; Carbohydrates: 30 g; Fats: 9 g; Fiber: 6 g; Cholesterol: 0 mg; Sodium: 150 mg; Potassium: 450 mg

# Tomato and Barley Soup with Thyme

*Prep. time: 10 min | Cook time: 30 min | Serves: 2*

Ingredients:
- ½ cup pearl barley, rinsed
- 2 cups low-sodium vegetable broth
- 1 cup canned diced tomatoes
- ½ cup carrots, diced
- ½ cup celery, diced
- ¼ cup onion, finely chopped
- 1 clove garlic, minced
- 1 tsp olive oil
- ½ tsp dried thyme
- ¼ tsp black pepper
- 1 tbsp fresh parsley, chopped (for garnish)

Directions:
6. Heat olive oil in a medium-sized pot over medium heat. Add onion, garlic, carrots and celery. Sauté for 5 minutes until vegetables are softened and fragrant.
7. Stir in the barley, thyme and black pepper. Cook for 1 minute to toast barley lightly.
8. Pour in diced tomatoes and vegetable broth. Stir to combine. Bring soup to a boil, then reduce heat to low. Cover and simmer for 25 minutes or until barley is tender. Taste and adjust seasoning, if needed.
9. Ladle soup into bowls and garnish with fresh parsley.

Nutritional Information (per serving): Calories: 180 kcal; Protein: 6 g; Carbohydrates: 32 g; Fats: 3 g; Fiber: 6 g; Cholesterol: 0 mg; Sodium: 100 mg; Potassium: 450 mg

# Roasted Beet and Avocado Salad

*Prep. time: 10 min | Cook time: 40 min | Serves: 2*

Ingredients:
- 4 cups mixed salad greens
- 2 medium beets, peeled and cut into wedges
- 1 small avocado, sliced
- ¼ cup red onion, thinly sliced
- 2 tbsp walnuts, toasted and chopped
- 2 tbsp fresh parsley, chopped
- 1 tbsp olive oil
- 1 tbsp balsamic vinegar
- 1 tsp Dijon mustard
- ¼ tsp black pepper

Directions:
1. Preheat oven to 200°C (400°F). Place beet wedges on a baking sheet lined with parchment paper. Drizzle with 1 tsp of olive oil and toss to coat. Roast for 35–40 minutes, flipping halfway through, until tender and slightly caramelized. Remove and let cool.
2. In a small bowl, whisk together olive oil, balsamic vinegar, Dijon mustard and black pepper.
3. In a large mixing bowl, combine mixed salad greens, roasted beets, avocado slices and red onion. Drizzle dressing over the salad and toss gently to coat.
4. Divide salad between two plates. Garnish with chopped walnuts and fresh parsley and serve.

Nutritional Information (per serving): Calories: 220 kcal; Protein: 5 g; Carbohydrates: 21 g; Fats: 14 g; Fiber: 7 g; Cholesterol: 0 mg; Sodium: 70 mg; Potassium: 550 mg

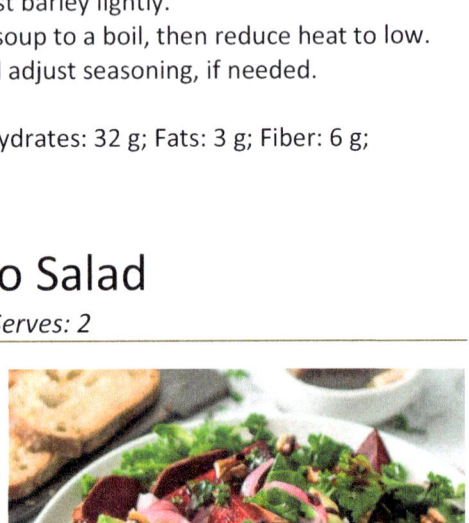

# Summer Gazpacho with Fresh Herbs

*Prep. time: 15 min | Chilling Time: 30 minutes | Serves: 2*

Ingredients:
- 2 large ripe tomatoes, chopped
- ½ cucumber, peeled and diced
- ½ red bell pepper, chopped
- ¼ cup red onion, finely chopped
- 1 small clove garlic, minced
- 1 cup low-sodium vegetable juice or tomato juice
- 1 tbsp olive oil
- 1 tbsp red wine vinegar
- 1 tbsp fresh basil or parsley, chopped
- ¼ tsp black pepper
- Pinch of salt (optional)

Directions:
1. Chop tomatoes, cucumber, red bell pepper and red onion into small pieces. Mince garlic.
2. In a blender, combine tomatoes, cucumber, red bell pepper, onion, garlic, vegetable juice, olive oil and red wine vinegar. Blend until smooth.
3. Add fresh basil or parsley, black pepper and a pinch of salt, if using. Blend briefly to incorporate herbs.
4. Transfer gazpacho to a large bowl or container. Cover and refrigerate for at least 30 minutes.
5. Stir chilled gazpacho before serving. Ladle into bowls or glasses and garnish with additional chopped herbs.

Nutritional Information (per serving): Calories: 120 kcal; Protein: 3 g; Carbohydrates: 14 g; Fats: 5 g; Fiber: 3 g; Cholesterol: 0 mg; Sodium: 95 mg; Potassium: 500 mg

# Herb-Roasted Potato Salad (No Mayo)

*Prep. time: 10 min | Cook time: 30 min | Serves: 2*

Ingredients:
- 2 cups baby potatoes, halved
- 1 tbsp olive oil
- ½ tsp garlic powder
- ¼ tsp black pepper
- 1 tsp Dijon mustard
- 1 tbsp fresh lemon juice
- 1 tsp fresh dill, chopped
- ¼ cup red onion, thinly sliced
- 1 tbsp capers
- Pinch of salt (optional)

Directions:
1. Preheat oven to 200°C (400°F). In a mixing bowl, toss halved baby potatoes with olive oil, garlic powder and black pepper. Spread them in a single layer on a baking sheet lined with parchment paper.
2. Roast potatoes in the oven for 25–30 minutes, flipping halfway through, until golden brown and tender.
3. In a small bowl whisk together Dijon mustard, lemon juice and a pinch of salt, if using.
4. Once potatoes are roasted and cooled slightly, transfer them to a bowl and toss gently with dressing.
5. Add fresh dill, red onion and capers. Toss again to combine.
6. Divide salad into two bowls. Serve warm or at room temperature.

Nutritional Information (per serving): Calories: 180 kcal; Protein: 3 g; Carbohydrates: 26 g; Fats: 7 g; Fiber: 4 g; Cholesterol: 0 mg; Sodium: 80 mg; Potassium: 450 mg

# Quinoa and Kale Detox Soup
*Prep. time: 10 min | Cook time: 25 min | Serves: 2*

Ingredients:
- ¼ cup quinoa, rinsed
- 2 cups low-sodium vegetable broth
- 1 cup kale, chopped
- ½ cup carrots, diced
- ½ cup celery, diced
- ¼ cup onion, finely chopped
- 1 clove garlic, minced
- 1 tsp olive oil
- ¼ tsp turmeric powder
- ¼ tsp black pepper
- ¼ tsp smoked paprika
- 1 tsp lemon juice
- 1 tbsp fresh parsley, chopped (for garnish)

Directions:
1. Heat olive oil in a medium pot over medium heat. Add onion and garlic, sautéing for 2 minutes until fragrant.
2. Stir in carrots, celery, turmeric, black pepper and smoked paprika. Cook for 3 minutes, stirring occasionally.
3. Add quinoa and vegetable broth. Bring to a boil, then reduce heat to low, cover and simmer for 15 minutes.
4. Stir in chopped kale and cook for an additional 3 minutes, just until wilted.
5. Remove soup from the heat and stir in lemon juice. Taste and adjust seasoning as needed.
6. Divide soup between two bowls. Garnish with fresh parsley and serve.

Nutritional Information (per serving): Calories: 150 kcal; Protein: 5 g; Carbohydrates: 22 g; Fats: 3 g; Fiber: 4 g; Cholesterol: 0 mg; Sodium: 90 mg; Potassium: 400 mg

# Mixed Greens with Orange and Pumpkin Seeds
*Prep. time: 10 min | Cook time: 0 min | Serves: 2*

Ingredients:
- 4 cups mixed salad greens
- 1 medium orange, peeled and segmented
- ¼ cup cucumber, thinly sliced
- ¼ cup red onion, thinly sliced
- 2 tbsp pumpkin seeds, toasted
- 1 tbsp olive oil
- 1 tbsp fresh orange juice
- 1 tsp balsamic vinegar
- ¼ tsp Dijon mustard
- ¼ tsp black pepper
- 1 tbsp dried cranberries (for garnish)

Directions:
1. In a small bowl, whisk together olive oil, orange juice, balsamic vinegar, Dijon mustard and black pepper.
2. In a large mixing bowl, combine mixed greens, orange segments, cucumber and red onion.
3. Sprinkle toasted pumpkin seeds over the salad. Drizzle dressing over the greens and toss gently to coat.
4. Divide salad between two plates. Garnish with dried cranberries and serve.

Nutritional Information (per serving): Calories: 150 kcal; Protein: 4 g; Carbohydrates: 12 g; Fats: 9 g; Fiber: 4 g; Cholesterol: 0 mg; Sodium: 20 mg; Potassium: 400 mg

# Roasted Garlic and Mushroom Soup

*Prep. time: 10 min | Chilling Time: 45 min | Serves: 2*

Ingredients:
- 2 cups button or cremini mushrooms, sliced
- 2 cups low-sodium vegetable broth
- ½ cup unsweetened almond milk
- 1 small head of garlic
- 1 small onion, diced
- 2 tsp olive oil, divided
- ½ tsp dried thyme
- ¼ tsp black pepper
- ¼ tsp smoked paprika
- 1 tbsp fresh parsley, chopped (for garnish)

Directions:
1. Preheat oven to 200°C (400°F). Slice the top off the garlic head, drizzle with 1 tsp of olive oil, wrap in foil and roast for 25–30 minutes until soft. Set aside to cool (can be done in advance the night before).
2. Heat 1 tsp of olive oil in a medium pot over medium heat. Add onion and sauté for 3–4 minutes, then add mushrooms, thyme, black pepper and smoked paprika. Cook for 5–7 minutes until mushrooms are tender.
3. Squeeze roasted garlic cloves into the pot, add vegetable broth, bring to a boil, then simmer for 10 minutes.
4. Remove pot from the heat and let soup cool slightly. Use an immersion blender to purée soup until smooth. Stir in almond milk and return to low heat, reheating gently. Adjust seasoning to taste.
5. Divide soup between two bowls, garnish with parsley and serve.

Nutritional Information (per serving): Calories: 120 kcal; Protein: 4 g; Carbohydrates: 14 g; Fats: 4 g; Fiber: 3 g; Cholesterol: 0 mg; Sodium: 90 mg; Potassium: 400 mg

# Warm Roasted Vegetable Salad with Balsamic Glaze

*Prep. time: 10 min | Cook time: 25 min | Serves: 2*

Ingredients:
- 2 cups mixed salad greens
- 1 cup broccoli florets
- 1 cup butternut squash, cubed
- 1 small zucchini, sliced
- ½ red bell pepper, sliced
- ¼ cup red onion, sliced
- 1 tbsp olive oil
- ½ tsp dried oregano
- 1 tbsp balsamic glaze
- 1 tbsp pumpkin seeds

Directions:
1. Preheat oven to 200°C (400°F). Line a baking sheet with parchment paper.
2. In a large mixing bowl, toss broccoli, butternut squash, zucchini, red bell pepper and red onion with olive oil and dried oregano.
3. Spread seasoned vegetables evenly on the prepared baking sheet. Roast in the oven for 20–25 minutes, stirring halfway through, until vegetables are tender and slightly caramelized.
4. Divide mixed salad greens between two plates. Top each serving with warm roasted vegetables.
5. Drizzle with balsamic glaze, sprinkle with pumpkin seeds and serve.

Nutritional Information (per serving): Calories: 190 kcal; Protein: 4 g; Carbohydrates: 18 g; Fats: 10 g; Fiber: 5 g; Cholesterol: 0 mg; Sodium: 60 mg; Potassium: 600 mg

# Cauliflower and Leek Soup with Garlic Croutons
*Prep. time: 10 min | Cook Time: 25 min | Serves: 2*

Ingredients:
- 2 cups cauliflower florets
- 2 cups low-sodium vegetable broth
- ½ cup unsweetened almond milk
- 1 medium leek (white and light green parts), thinly sliced
- 2 clove garlic, minced and divided
- 2 tsp olive oil, divided
- ¼ tsp black pepper
- ¼ tsp smoked paprika
- 1 slice whole-grain bread, cut into cubes
- ¼ tsp dried parsley

Directions:
1. Heat 1 tsp of olive oil in a medium pot over medium heat, sauté leek and half of minced garlic for 4 minutes.
2. Add cauliflower florets, vegetable broth, black pepper and smoked paprika to the pot. Bring to a boil, then reduce heat to low and simmer for 15 minutes or until cauliflower is tender.
3. Remove pot from the heat and let soup cool slightly. Using an immersion blender, blend soup until smooth.
4. Stir in almond milk and adjust seasoning if needed. Reheat gently, if required.
5. Heat a skillet over medium heat. Toss bread cubes with 1 tsp of olive oil and remaining minced garlic. Toast bread cubes in the skillet, stirring frequently, until golden brown and crisp. Sprinkle with dried parsley.
6. Ladle soup into bowls and top with croutons. Garnish with a sprinkle of fresh herbs, if desired and serve.

Nutritional Information (per serving): Calories: 160 kcal; Protein: 5 g; Carbohydrates: 18 g; Fats: 6 g; Fiber: 4 g; Cholesterol: 0 mg; Sodium: 110 mg; Potassium: 500 mg

# Zesty Bean and Corn Salad
*Prep. time: 15 min | Cook time: 0 min | Serves: 2*

Ingredients:
- 1 cup canned black beans, rinsed and drained
- 1 cup canned sweetcorn kernels, rinsed and drained
- 1 small red bell pepper, diced
- ¼ cup red onion, finely chopped
- 1 small avocado, diced
- 2 tbsp fresh lime juice
- 2 tbsp fresh cilantro, chopped
- 1 tbsp olive oil
- 1 clove garlic, minced
- ¼ tsp cumin powder
- Black pepper and salt to taste (optional)

Directions:
1. In a large mixing bowl, combine black beans, sweet corn, diced red bell pepper and red onion. Gently fold in avocado to avoid mashing.
2. In a small bowl, whisk together lime juice, chopped cilantro, olive oil, minced garlic, cumin, black pepper and salt, if using.
3. Pour dressing over the salad and toss gently to combine all ingredients evenly.
4. Divide salad between two bowls or plates. Garnish with additional cilantro and serve.

Nutritional Information (per serving): Calories: 220 kcal; Protein: 7 g; Carbohydrates: 28 g; Fats: 8 g; Fiber: 9 g; Cholesterol: 0 mg; Sodium: 60 mg; Potassium: 550 mg

# Split Pea Soup with Fresh Herbs

*Prep. time: 10 min | Cook Time: 40 min | Serves: 2*

Ingredients:
- ½ cup dried split peas, rinsed and drained
- 2 cups low-sodium vegetable broth
- 1 small onion, finely chopped
- 1 small carrot, diced
- 1 stalk celery, diced
- 2 cloves garlic, minced
- 1 tsp olive oil
- ½ tsp dried thyme
- ¼ tsp black pepper
- ½ tsp lemon juice
- 1 tbsp fresh parsley, chopped (for garnish)

Directions:
1. Heat 1 tsp of olive oil in a medium pot over medium heat. Add onion, carrot, celery and garlic. Sauté for 5 minutes until softened and fragrant.
2. Add rinsed split peas, vegetable broth, 1 cup of water, thyme and black pepper to the pot. Bring to a boil, then reduce heat to low. Cover and simmer for 35–40 minutes, stirring occasionally, until split peas are tender, and soup thickens.
3. For a smoother texture, use an immersion blender to partially blend the soup, leaving some texture intact.
4. Stir in lemon juice for added brightness. Adjust seasoning to taste.
5. Ladle soup into two bowls, garnish with fresh parsley and serve.

Nutritional Information (per serving): Calories: 180 kcal; Protein: 10 g; Carbohydrates: 30 g; Fats: 3 g; Fiber: 9 g; Cholesterol: 0 mg; Sodium: 120 mg; Potassium: 450 mg

# Spinach and Strawberry Salad with Balsamic Glaze

*Prep. time: 10 min | Cook time: 0 min | Serves: 2*

Ingredients:
- 4 cups fresh spinach, washed and dried
- 1 cup fresh strawberries, sliced
- ¼ cup red onion, thinly sliced
- ¼ cup walnuts, roughly chopped
- 2 tbsp sunflower seeds
- 2 tbsp balsamic glaze
- 1 tbsp olive oil
- ¼ tsp black pepper
- 1 tbsp fresh mint or basil leaves, chopped (for garnish)

Directions:
1. Wash and dry spinach, slice strawberries and thinly slice red onion.
   Toast walnuts in a dry skillet over medium heat for 2–3 minutes until golden brown.
2. Place spinach in a large salad bowl. Top with sliced strawberries, red onion, toasted walnuts and sunflower seeds.
3. In a small bowl, whisk together olive oil, balsamic glaze and black pepper.
4. Drizzle dressing over salad and toss gently to coat. Garnish with fresh mint or basil and serve immediately.

Nutritional Information (per serving): Calories: 190 kcal; Protein: 4 g; Carbohydrates: 15 g; Fats: 12 g; Fiber: 4 g; Cholesterol: 0 mg; Sodium: 40 mg; Potassium: 450 mg

# Low-Cholesterol Main Dishes

# Quinoa-Stuffed Bell Peppers with Chickpeas

*Prep. time: 10 min | Cook Time: 35 min | Serves: 2*

Ingredients:
- 2 large bell peppers, halved and seeds removed
- ½ cup quinoa, cooked
- ½ cup canned chickpeas, rinsed and drained
- ¼ cup canned diced tomatoes
- ¼ cup zucchini, finely diced
- ¼ cup onion, finely chopped
- 1 clove garlic, minced
- ½ tsp cumin
- ½ tsp smoked paprika
- 1 tbsp olive oil, divided
- 1 tbsp fresh parsley, chopped (for garnish)
- Pinch of salt

Directions:
1. Preheat oven to 200°C (400°F). Place halved bell peppers on a baking dish, drizzle with ½ tbsp of olive oil and roast for 10 minutes until slightly softened.
2. Heat the remaining ½ tbsp of olive oil in a skillet over medium heat. Add onion and garlic, sauté for 3–4 minutes until softened. Stir in zucchini, diced tomatoes, chickpeas, cumin and smoked paprika. Cook for 5 minutes. Add cooked quinoa and a pinch of salt. Mix well and cook for an additional 2 minutes.
3. Remove roasted bell peppers from the oven and carefully fill each half with the quinoa-chickpea mixture. Return to the oven and bake for another 15 minutes.
4. Remove from the oven, garnish with fresh parsley and serve.

Nutritional Information (per serving): Calories: 250 kcal; Protein: 7 g; Carbohydrates: 30 g; Fats: 9 g; Fiber: 7 g; Cholesterol: 0 mg; Sodium: 100 mg; Potassium: 450 mg

# Sweet Potato and Lentil Curry

*Prep. time: 10 min | Cook time: 25 min | Serves: 2*

Ingredients:
- 1 medium sweet potato, peeled and diced
- ½ cup dried red lentils, rinsed
- ½ cup canned diced tomatoes
- 1 cup coconut milk
- 1 cup low sodium vegetable broth
- 1 tbsp olive oil
- ½ small onion, finely chopped
- 1 clove garlic, minced
- ½ tsp turmeric
- ½ tsp cumin

Directions:
1. Heat olive oil in a medium pot over medium heat. Add chopped onion and garlic and sauté for 2–3 minutes.
2. Stir in turmeric and cumin and cook for 30 seconds. Add diced sweet potato and stir to coat with spices.
3. Add lentils, diced tomatoes, coconut milk and vegetable broth. Bring to a boil, then reduce heat to a simmer. Cover and cook for 20 minutes, stirring occasionally, until sweet potato is tender, and lentils are soft.
4. Divide curry between two bowls. Garnish with a sprinkle of fresh herbs, if desired and serve.

Nutritional Information (per serving): Calories: 300 kcal; Protein: 9 g; Carbohydrates: 40 g; Fats: 10 g; Fiber: 10 g; Cholesterol: 0 mg; Sodium: 100 mg; Potassium: 700 mg

# Baked Eggplant Parmesan (Dairy-Free)

*Prep. time: 15 min | Cook Time: 45 min | Serves: 2*

Ingredients:
- 1 medium eggplant, sliced into ½-inch rounds
- ½ cup unsweetened almond milk
- 1 cup low sodium marinara sauce
- 1 cup whole-grain breadcrumbs
- ¼ cup nutritional yeast
- 1 tsp Italian seasoning
- ½ tsp garlic powder
- ¼ tsp black pepper
- 1 tbsp olive oil
- ¼ cup fresh basil, chopped (for garnish)

Directions:
1. Preheat oven to 200°C (400°F). Lightly salt eggplant slices and let them sit for 10 minutes to draw out excess moisture. Pat them dry with a paper towel.
2. In one bowl, add almond milk. In another bowl, mix breadcrumbs, nutritional yeast, Italian seasoning, garlic powder and black pepper. Dip eggplant slices into almond milk, then coat evenly with breadcrumb mixture.
3. Arrange breaded eggplant slices on a parchment-lined baking sheet. Drizzle lightly with olive oil. Bake for 20 minutes, then flip slices and bake for an additional 15 minutes until golden brown and crispy.
4. Spread a thin layer of marinara sauce at the bottom of a baking dish, followed by the layer of baked eggplant slices. Repeat the layers until all eggplant and sauce are used. Return to oven and bake for 10 minutes.
5. Remove from the oven and garnish with fresh basil. Serve warm with a side salad or steamed vegetables.

Nutritional Information (per serving): Calories: 250 kcal; Protein: 7 g; Carbohydrates: 30 g; Fats: 9 g; Fiber: 8 g; Cholesterol: 0 mg; Sodium: 120 mg; Potassium: 650 mg

# Roasted Cauliflower Steaks with Chimichurri

*Prep. time: 10 min | Cook time: 30 min | Serves: 2*

Ingredients:
- 1 large cauliflower head, trimmed and cut into 1-inch thick "steaks"
- 5 tbsp olive oil, divided
- ½ tsp smoked paprika
- ½ tsp garlic powder
- ¼ tsp black pepper
- ½ cup fresh parsley or cilantro, finely chopped
- 1 clove garlic, minced
- 2 tbsp red wine vinegar
- ½ tsp red chili flakes (optional)
- ¼ tsp salt

Directions:
1. Preheat oven to 200°C (400°F). Cut cauliflower into 1-inch thick "steaks". Brush both sides of the steaks with 2 tbsp of olive oil. Sprinkle smoked paprika, garlic powder and black pepper evenly over both sides.
2. Roast on a parchment-lined baking sheet for 25–30 minutes, flipping halfway, until golden and tender.
3. In a small bowl, mix parsley, minced garlic, remaining olive oil, vinegar, chili flakes and salt. Stir to combine.
4. Plate roasted cauliflower steaks and spoon sauce generously over the top.
5. Serve immediately with a side of quinoa or a fresh green salad for a complete meal.

Nutritional Information (per serving): Calories: 230 kcal; Protein: 4 g; Carbohydrates: 10 g; Fats: 19 g; Fiber: 5 g; Cholesterol: 0 mg; Sodium: 110 mg; Potassium: 580 mg

# Teriyaki Tofu Stir-Fry with Brown Rice

*Prep. time: 10 min | Cook Time: 20 min | Serves: 2*

Ingredients:
- 1 block (225gm/8oz) firm tofu, pressed and cubed
- 1 cup broccoli florets
- 1 medium red bell pepper, sliced
- 1 medium carrot, julienned
- 2 cups cooked brown rice
- 3 tbsp low-sodium soy sauce
- 1 tbsp maple syrup or honey
- 1 tsp sesame oil
- 1 tsp cornstarch, dissolved in 2 tbsp water
- 1 tbsp olive oil, divided

Directions:
1. Heat ½ tbsp of olive oil in a non-stick skillet over medium heat. Add tofu cubes and cook for 3–4 minutes per side until golden brown. Remove and set aside.
2. In the same skillet, heat the remaining ½ tbsp of olive oil over medium-high heat. Add broccoli, red bell pepper and carrot. Stir-fry for 5–6 minutes until tender-crisp.
3. In a small bowl, mix soy sauce, maple syrup, sesame oil and cornstarch slurry. Pour sauce into the skillet and stir until it thickens slightly, about 1–2 minutes.
4. Return tofu to the skillet and toss to coat with sauce and vegetables. Serve stir-fry over warm brown rice.

Nutritional Information (per serving): Calories: 340 kcal; Protein: 12 g; Carbohydrates: 50 g; Fats: 8 g; Fiber: 5 g; Cholesterol: 0 mg; Sodium: 280 mg; Potassium: 580 mg

# Vegan Shepherd's Pie with Lentils and Sweet Potato

*Prep. time: 15 min | Cook time: 45 min | Serves: 2*

Ingredients:
- 2 medium sweet potatoes, peeled and cubed
- 2 tbsp unsweetened almond milk
- ¼ tsp black pepper
- 1 tbsp olive oil
- 1 small onion, diced
- 1 medium carrot, diced
- 1 cup cooked lentils
- ½ cup vegetable stock
- 1 tbsp tomato paste
- ½ tsp smoked paprika

Directions:
1. Bring a pot of water to a boil. Add cubed sweet potatoes and cook for 10–12 minutes or until tender. Drain and mash sweet potatoes with almond milk, ½ tbsp of olive oil and black pepper. Set aside.
2. Heat the remaining olive oil in a skillet over medium heat. Sauté diced onion and carrot for 5–7 minutes until softened, then stir in lentils, tomato paste, smoked paprika and stock. Simmer for 8–10 minutes until thickened.
3. Preheat oven to 200°C (400°F). Spread lentil filling evenly in a small baking dish. Top with mashed sweet potato, spreading it evenly over the filling. Use a fork to create ridges on the surface for texture.
4. Bake for 20–25 minutes or until topping is lightly golden and crisp. Let cool for 5 minutes before serving

Nutritional Information (per serving): Calories: 320 kcal; Protein: 10 g; Carbohydrates: 52 g; Fats: 5 g; Fiber: 10 g; Cholesterol: 0 mg; Sodium: 180 mg; Potassium: 700 mg

# Stuffed Portobello Mushrooms with Brown Rice

*Prep. time: 15 min | Cook Time: 25 min | Serves: 2*

Ingredients:
- 4 large portobello mushrooms, stems removed
- 1 cup cooked brown rice
- 1 small onion, finely diced
- 1 medium red bell pepper, finely diced
- 1 tbsp olive oil, divided
- 1 clove garlic, minced
- ½ tsp smoked paprika
- ½ tsp dried oregano
- ¼ cup fresh parsley, chopped and divided
- 1 tbsp sunflower seeds
- Salt and black pepper, to taste

Directions:
1. Preheat oven to 200°C (400°F). Clean portobello mushrooms with a damp paper towel and remove stems. Lightly brush mushrooms with ½ tbsp of olive oil and place them on a baking sheet, gill-side up.
2. Heat the remaining olive oil in a skillet over medium heat. Sauté onion, bell pepper and garlic for 5–7 minutes. Stir in rice, smoked paprika, oregano, half of the parsley, salt and pepper. Cook for 2–3 minutes.
3. Fill mushrooms with rice mixture, gently pressing the filling into each cap. Sprinkle sunflower seeds on top.
4. Bake stuffed mushrooms in the preheated oven for 15–18 minutes or until mushrooms are tender.

*Serve with steamed or roasted vegetables or a green salad for a complete and nutritious meal.

Nutritional Information (per serving): Calories: 230 kcal; Protein: 7 g; Carbohydrates: 30 g; Fats: 8 g; Fiber: 5 g; Cholesterol: 0 mg; Sodium: 120 mg; Potassium: 750 mg

# Moroccan Chickpea and Vegetable Tagine

*Prep. time: 10 min | Cook time: 30 min | Serves: 2*

Ingredients:
- ½ cup carrots, diced
- ½ cup zucchini, diced
- ½ cup canned chickpeas, rinsed and drained
- ½ cup canned diced tomatoes
- ½ cup low-sodium vegetable broth
- 1 tbsp olive oil
- ½ cup onion, diced
- 2 cloves garlic, minced
- ½ tsp ground cumin
- ½ tsp ground cinnamon
- 2 tbsp fresh cilantro, chopped (for garnish)

Directions:
1. Heat olive oil in a medium skillet over medium heat. Add onion and sauté for 3-4 minutes, then add garlic and cook for 1 minute. Stir in cumin and cinnamon and cook for 30 seconds to release their aroma.
2. Add carrots, zucchini, chickpeas and canned tomatoes. Stir to coat vegetables in the spices.
3. Pour in vegetable broth and bring to a gentle boil. Reduce heat to low, cover and simmer for 20-25 minutes, stirring occasionally, until vegetables are tender. Taste and adjust seasoning.
4. Spoon tagine into bowls, garnish with chopped cilantro and serve.

Nutritional Information (per serving): Calories: 230 kcal; Protein: 7 g; Carbohydrates: 30 g; Fats: 8 g; Fiber: 5 g; Cholesterol: 0 mg; Sodium: 120 mg; Potassium: 750 mg

# Grilled Tofu Skewers with Peanut Sauce

*Prep. time: 15 min | Cook Time: 10 min | Serves: 2*

Ingredients:
- 1 block (225gm/8oz) extra-firm tofu, cubed
- ½ cup red bell pepper, diced
- ½ cup zucchini, sliced into rounds
- 1 tbsp olive oil
- ½ tsp smoked paprika
- ¼ tsp black pepper
- 2 tbsp unsweetened peanut butter
- 1 tbsp low-sodium soy sauce
- 1 tbsp fresh lime juice
- 1 tsp maple syrup

Directions:
1. Press tofu between paper towels to remove excess moisture, then cut into 1-inch cubes.
2. In a bowl, toss tofu cubes, bell pepper and zucchini with olive oil, smoked paprika and black pepper.
3. Thread tofu, bell pepper and zucchini onto skewers, alternating the ingredients for an even mix.
4. Heat a grill pan over medium heat. Grill skewers for 8-10 minutes, turning occasionally, until vegetables are slightly charred, and tofu is golden brown.
5. In a small bowl, whisk together peanut butter, soy sauce, lime juice, maple syrup and 1 tbsp of water until smooth. Adjust consistency with more water, if needed.
6. Arrange skewers on a plate and drizzle with peanut sauce, serve over a bed of quinoa or brown rice.

Nutritional Information (per serving): Calories: 300 kcal; Protein: 13 g; Carbohydrates: 12 g; Fats: 22 g; Fiber: 3 g; Cholesterol: 0 mg; Sodium: 220 mg; Potassium: 650 mg

# Roasted Vegetable Buddha Bowl with Tahini Dressing

*Prep. time: 10 min | Cook time: 30 min | Serves: 2*

Ingredients:
- 1 cup cooked quinoa (approx. ⅓ cup dry quinoa)
- 1 cup sweet potato, diced
- 1 cup broccoli florets
- ½ cup red bell pepper, diced
- 1 tbsp olive oil
- ½ tsp smoked paprika
- ¼ tsp ground cumin
- 2 tbsp tahini
- 1 tbsp fresh lemon juice
- 1 tsp maple syrup
- 1 clove garlic, minced

Directions:
1. Cook quinoa according to package instructions. Fluff and set aside.
2. Preheat oven to 200°C (400°F). On a baking sheet, toss diced sweet potato, broccoli florets and red bell pepper with olive oil, smoked paprika and cumin. Spread evenly.
3. Roast for 25-30 minutes, flipping halfway, until vegetables are tender and slightly caramelized.
4. In a small bowl, whisk together tahini, lemon juice, maple syrup, minced garlic and 1 tbsp of water.
5. Divide quinoa between two bowls, top with roasted vegetables, drizzle with tahini dressing and serve.

Nutritional Information (per serving): Calories: 350 kcal; Protein: 9 g; Carbohydrates: 48 g; Fats: 13 g; Fiber: 8 g; Cholesterol: 0 mg; Sodium: 140 mg; Potassium: 900 mg

# Cauliflower Fried Rice with Tofu

*Prep. time: 10 min | Cook time: 15 min | Serves: 2*

Ingredients:
- 2 cups cauliflower rice, grated from fresh cauliflower
- 1 block (225gm/8oz) extra-firm tofu, cubed
- ½ cup frozen peas and carrots, thawed
- ½ cup broccoli florets, chopped
- ¼ cup red bell pepper, diced
- 1 clove garlic, minced
- 1 tbsp low-sodium soy sauce or tamari
- 1 tsp sesame oil, divided
- ¼ tsp black pepper
- 1 tbsp green onions, sliced (for garnish)

Directions:
1. Press tofu between paper towels to remove excess moisture, then cut into 1-inch cubes.
2. Heat ½ tsp of sesame oil in a large skillet or wok over medium heat. Add tofu cubes and cook for 5-7 minutes, turning occasionally, until golden brown on all sides. Remove from the skillet and set aside.
3. Add the remaining sesame oil to the same skillet. Stir-fry garlic, broccoli, bell pepper, peas and carrots for 3–4 minutes. Add cauliflower rice, season with black pepper and cook for 3–4 minutes until tender.
4. Return tofu to the skillet, drizzle with soy sauce and toss everything to combine. Cook for 1-2 minutes.
5. Divide cauliflower fried rice into two bowls. Garnish with sliced green onions and enjoy warm.

Nutritional Information (per serving): Calories: 250 kcal; Protein: 12 g; Carbohydrates: 18 g; Fats: 9 g; Fiber: 6 g; Cholesterol: 0 mg; Sodium: 280 mg; Potassium: 700 mg

# Baked Cod with Lemon and Herbs

*Prep. time: 10 min | Cook time: 15 min | Serves: 2*

Ingredients:
- 2 cod fillets
- 1 cup cherry tomatoes, halved
- 1 tbsp olive oil
- 1 tbsp fresh lemon juice
- 1 tsp lemon zest
- 2 cloves garlic, minced
- 1 tbsp fresh parsley, chopped
- ½ tsp dried thyme
- ½ tsp paprika
- ¼ tsp salt (optional)

Directions:
1. Preheat oven to 200°C (400°F). Lightly grease a baking dish with a small amount of olive oil or cooking spray.
2. Pat cod fillets dry with a paper towel. In a small bowl, mix olive oil, lemon juice, lemon zest, minced garlic, parsley, thyme, paprika and salt. Brush or rub mixture evenly over both sides of the cod fillets.
3. Arrange cherry tomatoes around the cod in the baking dish. Toss lightly with olive oil and black pepper.
4. Place baking dish in the preheated oven and bake for 12-15 minutes or until cod flakes easily with a fork.
5. Plate cod fillets alongside the roasted cherry tomatoes. Garnish with additional fresh parsley and a wedge of lemon. Serve with a side of quinoa or brown rice and steamed green beans for a balanced meal.

Nutritional Information (per serving): Calories: 220 kcal; Protein: 28 g; Carbohydrates: 6 g; Fats: 8 g; Fiber: 2 g; Cholesterol: 55 mg; Sodium: 170 mg; Potassium: 780 mg Calories: 220 kcal; Protein: 28 g; Carbohydrates: 6 g; Fats: 8 g; Fiber: 2 g; Cholesterol: 55 mg; Sodium: 170 mg; Potassium: 780 mg

# Vegan Bolognese with Whole-Grain Pasta

*Prep. time: 10 min | Cook Time: 20 min | Serves: 2*

Ingredients:
- 115 gm (4oz) whole-grain pasta, spaghetti or penne
- 1 cup mushrooms, finely chopped
- ½ cup carrots, finely diced
- ½ cup celery, finely diced
- ½ cup canned crushed tomatoes
- ¼ cup red onion, finely diced
- 2 cloves garlic, minced
- 1 tbsp olive oil
- ½ tsp dried oregano
- ½ tsp dried basil
- ¼ tsp black pepper

Directions:
1. Cook whole-grain pasta according to package instructions until al dente. Drain and set aside.
2. Heat olive oil in a large skillet over medium heat. Add red onion and garlic, and sauté for 2 minutes until fragrant. Add carrots, celery and mushrooms. Cook for 5-6 minutes, stirring occasionally, until softened.
3. Stir in the crushed tomatoes, oregano, basil and black pepper. Simmer for 10 minutes, stirring occasionally, until sauce thickens.
4. Toss cooked pasta with Bolognese sauce in the skillet. Stir well to coat pasta evenly.
5. Divide Bolognese into two bowls and serve

Nutritional Information (per serving): Calories: 320 kcal; Protein: 11 g; Carbohydrates: 55 g; Fats: 8 g; Fiber: 9 g; Cholesterol: 0 mg; Sodium: 140 mg; Potassium: 720 mg

# Baked Salmon with Garlic, Dill and Asparagus

*Prep. time: 10 min | Cook time: 15 min | Serves: 2*

Ingredients:
- 2 salmon fillets, skin-on
- 8-10 asparagus spears, trimmed
- ½ cup yellow squash or zucchini, sliced into rounds
- 1 tbsp olive oil
- 2 cloves garlic, minced
- 1 tbsp fresh dill, chopped
- 1 tbsp fresh lemon juice
- ½ tsp lemon zest
- ¼ tsp black pepper
- Pinch of salt (optional)

Directions:
1. Preheat oven to 200°C (400°F). Line a baking sheet with parchment paper.
2. Place salmon fillets on the baking sheet. Arrange asparagus and sliced squash or zucchini around salmon.
3. Drizzle olive oil and lemon juice over the salmon and vegetables. Sprinkle with minced garlic, fresh dill, lemon zest, black pepper and salt.
4. Bake in the preheated oven for 12-15 minutes, until salmon flakes with a fork and vegetables are tender.
5. Plate salmon with asparagus and yellow squash. Garnish with additional fresh dill and a lemon wedge.
6. Serve with a side of quinoa or steamed baby potatoes drizzled with olive oil and fresh herbs.

Nutritional Information (per serving): Calories: 310 kcal; Protein: 30 g; Carbohydrates: 8 g; Fats: 16 g; Fiber: 3 g; Cholesterol: 55 mg; Sodium: 120 mg; Potassium: 750 mg

# Roasted Eggplant and Chickpea Salad Bowl

*Prep. time: 10 min | Cook Time: 25 min | Serves: 2*

Ingredients:
- 2 cups mixed salad greens
- 1 medium eggplant, diced into 1-inch cubes
- 1 cup canned chickpeas, rinsed and drained
- 1 tbsp olive oil
- ½ tsp ground cumin
- ¼ tsp black pepper
- ½ cup cherry tomatoes, halved
- ¼ cup cucumber, diced
- 1 tbsp tahini
- 1 tbsp fresh lemon juice

Directions:
1. Preheat oven to 200°C (400°F). Line a baking sheet with parchment paper.
2. Toss eggplant and chickpeas with olive oil, ground cumin and black pepper. Spread on the baking sheet. Roast for 20-25 minutes, stirring occasionally, until eggplant is tender, and chickpeas are crispy.
3. In a small bowl, whisk tahini, lemon juice and 1 tbsp of water until smooth. Adjust water as needed.
4. Divide mixed salad greens between two bowls. Top with roasted eggplant, chickpeas, cherry tomatoes and cucumber. Drizzle tahini dressing over the salad.
5. Garnish with an extra squeeze of lemon juice or a sprinkle of fresh herbs, if desired, and serve immediately.

Nutritional Information (per serving): Calories: 310 kcal; Protein: 9 g; Carbohydrates: 32 g; Fats: 13 g; Fiber: 10 g; Cholesterol: 0 mg; Sodium: 200 mg; Potassium: 780 mg

# Sweet Potato and Black Bean Enchiladas

*Prep. time: 15 min | Cook time: 25 min | Serves: 2*

Ingredients:
- 4 small whole-grain tortillas
- 1 cup sweet potato, peeled and diced
- ½ cup canned black beans, rinsed and drained
- ½ cup low-sodium enchilada sauce
- ¼ cup red onion, finely diced
- 1 clove garlic, minced
- ½ tsp smoked paprika
- 1 tsp olive oil
- 1 tbsp nutritional yeast
- 2 tbsp fresh cilantro, chopped (for garnish)

Directions:
1. Heat olive oil in a skillet over medium heat. Add sweet potatoes and cook for 5-6 minutes, stirring occasionally, until softened.
2. Add red onion, garlic and smoked paprika to the skillet. Stir well and cook for 2 minutes. Add black beans and cook for another 2 minutes until heated through.
3. Preheat oven to 190°C (375°F). Spread 1-2 tbsp of enchilada sauce on the bottom of a small baking dish.
4. Fill each tortilla with sweet potato and black bean mixture, roll them up, and place seam-side down in the dish. Pour remaining enchilada sauce over the top and sprinkle with nutritional yeast.
5. Bake for 15 minutes, until heated through. Garnish with fresh cilantro and serve warm.

Nutritional Information (per serving): Calories: 320 kcal; Protein: 10 g; Carbohydrates: 55 g; Fats: 7 g; Fiber: 11 g; Cholesterol: 0 mg; Sodium: 340 mg; Potassium: 680 mg

# Butternut Squash and Kale Risotto

*Prep. time: 10 min | Cook Time: 30 min | Serves: 2*

Ingredients:
- ½ cup Arborio rice
- 1½ cups butternut squash, diced
- 2 cups low-sodium vegetable broth, warmed
- 1 cup kale, chopped
- ½ cup yellow onion, finely diced
- 2 cloves garlic, minced
- 1 tbsp olive oil
- ½ tsp dried thyme
- ¼ tsp black pepper
- 1 tbsp nutritional yeast
- 1 tsp fresh lemon juice

Directions:
1. Heat olive oil in a saucepan over medium heat. Sauté onion, garlic and butternut squash for 4-5 minutes.
2. Stir in Arborio rice and cook for 1-2 minutes, stirring frequently, until lightly toasted.
3. Gradually add warmed vegetable broth, 1/2 cup at a time, stirring often. Let the liquid absorb before adding more. Cook for 20-25 minutes until rice is creamy and squash is tender.
4. Stir in kale, thyme, black pepper and nutritional yeast. Cook for 2-3 minutes until kale wilts.
5. Finish with a squeeze of lemon juice and serve warm.

Nutritional Information (per serving): Calories: 310 kcal; Protein: 7 g; Carbohydrates: 50 g; Fats: 8 g; Fiber: 6 g; Cholesterol: 0 mg; Sodium: 170 mg; Potassium: 640 mg

# Hearty Vegetable and Lentil Stew

*Prep. time: 10 min | Cook time: 30 min | Serves: 2*

Ingredients:
- ½ cup dried green or brown lentils, rinsed
- 1 cup low-sodium vegetable broth
- ½ cup canned diced tomatoes
- ½ cup carrots, diced
- ½ cup celery, diced
- ½ cup zucchini, diced
- ¼ cup yellow onion, finely diced
- 1 clove garlic, minced
- 1 tsp olive oil
- ½ tsp dried thyme
- ¼ tsp smoked paprika
- ¼ tsp black pepper

Directions:
1. Heat olive oil in a medium pot over medium heat. Sauté onion and garlic for 2-3 minutes until softened.
2. Stir in carrots, celery, zucchini, thyme, smoked paprika and black pepper. Cook for 3-4 minutes.
3. Add lentils, vegetable broth, 1 cup of water and diced tomatoes. Stir to combine.
4. Bring to a gentle boil, then reduce heat to low. Cover and simmer for 25-30 minutes, stirring occasionally, until lentils and vegetables are tender.
5. Taste and adjust seasoning, if needed. Ladle into bowls and serve warm.

Nutritional Information (per serving): Calories: 240 kcal; Protein: 10 g; Carbohydrates: 35 g; Fats: 4 g; Fiber: 9 g; Cholesterol: 0 mg; Sodium: 160 mg; Potassium: 690 mg

# Broccoli and Cashew Stir-Fry with Brown Rice
*Prep. time: 10 min | Cook Time: 20 min | Serves: 2*

Ingredients:
- 1 cup brown rice, cooked (approx. ½ cup dry rice)
- 2 cups broccoli florets
- ½ cup red bell pepper, sliced
- ¼ cup unsalted cashews
- 1 clove garlic, minced
- 1 tsp fresh ginger, grated
- 1 tbsp olive oil or sesame oil
- 2 tbsp low-sodium soy sauce or tamari
- 1 tbsp fresh lime juice
- ¼ tsp black pepper

Directions:
1. Cook ½ cup of dry brown rice according to package instructions. Set aside.
2. Toast cashews in a dry skillet over medium heat for 2-3 minutes until golden and fragrant, and set aside.
3. Heat olive oil in a large skillet over medium heat. Add garlic and ginger, and sauté for 30 seconds until fragrant. Add broccoli and red bell pepper. Stir-fry for 5-7 minutes until vegetables are tender but still crisp.
4. Add soy sauce, lime juice and black pepper, tossing to coat. Stir in cashews and cook for 1–2 minutes.
5. Divide cooked brown rice between two plates. Top with broccoli and cashew stir-fry and serve.

Nutritional Information (per serving): Calories: 320 kcal; Protein: 8 g; Carbohydrates: 42 g; Fats: 12 g; Fiber: 6 g; Cholesterol: 0 mg; Sodium: 230 mg; Potassium: 540 mg

# Mushroom and Barley Stuffed Cabbage Rolls
*Prep. time: 20 min | Cook time: 35 min | Serves: 2*

Ingredients:
- 4 large cabbage leaves
- 1½ cups cooked pearl barley (approx. ½ cup dry pearl barley)
- 1 cup mushrooms, finely chopped
- ½ cup yellow onion, finely diced
- 2 cloves garlic, minced
- ½ tsp dried thyme
- ¼ tsp ground black pepper
- 1 tbsp olive oil
- 1 cup low-sodium tomato sauce
- 1 tsp balsamic vinegar
- 2 tbsp fresh parsley, chopped (for garnish)

Directions:
1. Bring a large pot of water to a boil. Carefully peel off 4 cabbage leaves and blanch them for 2-3 minutes.
2. Heat olive oil in a skillet over medium heat. Sauté onion and garlic for 2-3 minutes.
3. Add mushrooms, thyme and black pepper. Cook for 5-6 minutes, stirring occasionally, until mushrooms release their moisture. Stir in cooked barley and 2 tbsp of tomato sauce and cook for another 2 minutes.
4. Place mushroom and barley filling into the centre of cabbage leaves, fold and roll tightly.
5. Preheat oven to 190°C (375°F). Place cabbage rolls in a baking dish, pour the remaining tomato sauce and drizzle with balsamic vinegar. Cover with foil and bake for 20 minutes, then uncover and bake for 5 minutes.
6. Garnish with freshly chopped parsley before serving.

Nutritional Information (per serving): Calories: 280 kcal; Protein: 7 g; Carbohydrates: 45 g; Fats: 8 g; Fiber: 9 g; Cholesterol: 0 mg; Sodium: 180 mg; Potassium: 720 mg

# Cholesterol-Friendly Sides & Snacks

# Baked Sweet Potato Wedges with Smoked Paprika

*Prep. time: 10 min | Cook Time: 25 min | Serves: 2*

Ingredients:
- 2 medium sweet potatoes, scrubbed and cut into wedges
- 1 tbsp olive oil
- ½ tsp smoked paprika
- ¼ tsp ground cumin
- ¼ tsp garlic powder
- ¼ tsp black pepper
- ¼ tsp salt (optional)
- 1 tsp fresh parsley, chopped (for garnish)

Directions:
1. Preheat oven to 200°C (400°F). Line a baking sheet with parchment paper.
2. In a large bowl, toss sweet potato wedges with olive oil, smoked paprika, cumin, garlic powder, black pepper and salt, if using.
3. Spread seasoned wedges in a single layer on the prepared baking sheet.
4. Bake for 20-25 minutes, flipping halfway through, until wedges are golden and tender with crisp edges.
5. Transfer sweet potato wedges to a serving dish and sprinkle with fresh parsley.

   *Serve with a side of hummus, a yogurt-based dip or a fresh salad for a complete and nutritious meal.

Nutritional Information (per serving): Calories: 180 kcal; Protein: 2 g; Carbohydrates: 27 g; Fats: 7 g; Fiber: 4 g; Cholesterol: 0 mg; Sodium: 150 mg; Potassium: 450 mg

# Baked Polenta Fries with Marinara Dip

*Prep. time: 10 min | Cook time: 30 min | Serves: 2*

Ingredients:
- 1 cup precooked polenta (tube-style), cut into fry-shaped sticks
- ½ cup low-sodium marinara sauce
- 1 tbsp olive oil
- ½ tsp smoked paprika
- ½ tsp garlic powder
- ¼ tsp black pepper
- ¼ tsp salt (optional)
- ¼ tsp dried oregano
- ¼ tsp red chili flakes

Directions:
1. Preheat oven to 200°C (400°F). Line a baking sheet with parchment paper.
2. Slice precooked polenta into fry-shaped sticks, about ½ inch thick.
3. Place polenta sticks in a large bowl. Drizzle with olive oil and sprinkle with smoked paprika, garlic powder, black pepper and salt, if using. Toss gently to coat.
4. Arrange polenta sticks in a single layer on the prepared baking sheet.
5. Bake for 25-30 minutes, flipping halfway through, until fries are golden and crispy on the edges.
6. In a small saucepan over low heat, combine marinara sauce, dried oregano and red chili flakes. Warm for 3-5 minutes, stirring occasionally.
7. Transfer baked polenta fries to a serving plate and serve with warm marinara dip on the side.

Nutritional Information (per serving): Calories: 190 kcal; Protein: 4 g; Carbohydrates: 22 g; Fats: 8 g; Fiber: 3 g; Cholesterol: 0 mg; Sodium: 230 mg; Potassium: 150 mg

# Garlic and Herb Roasted Mushrooms

*Prep. time: 5 min | Cook time: 20 min | Serves: 2*

Ingredients:
- 8 oz button or cremini mushrooms, cleaned and halved
- 1 tbsp olive oil
- 2 cloves garlic, minced
- 1 tsp fresh thyme leaves
- 1 tsp fresh rosemary, finely chopped
- ¼ tsp black pepper
- ¼ tsp salt (optional)
- 1 tsp fresh lemon juice
- 1 tbsp fresh parsley, chopped (for garnish)

Directions:
1. Preheat oven to 200°C (400°F). Line a baking sheet with parchment paper.
2. In a large mixing bowl, toss mushrooms with olive oil, garlic, thyme, rosemary, black pepper and salt.
3. Spread seasoned mushrooms in a single layer on the prepared baking sheet.
4. Roast for 18-20 minutes, stirring halfway through, until mushrooms are tender and golden brown.
5. Remove from the oven and toss mushrooms with lemon juice. Sprinkle with fresh parsley before serving.

   *Can be served as a side dish with roasted vegetables or quinoa, or as a topping for whole-grain toast.

Nutritional Information (per serving): Calories: 110 kcal; Protein: 3 g; Carbohydrates: 5 g; Fats: 8 g; Fiber: 1 g; Cholesterol: 0 mg; Sodium: 100 mg; Potassium: 400 mg

# Baked Zucchini Sticks with Marinara Sauce

*Prep. time: 10 min | Cook Time: 20 min | Serves: 2*

Ingredients:
- 2 medium zucchinis, cut into sticks, about 3 inches long
- ½ cup whole-grain breadcrumbs or gluten-free alternative
- 2 tbsp nutritional yeast
- 1 tsp garlic powder
- ½ tsp smoked paprika
- ¼ tsp black pepper
- ¼ tsp salt (optional)
- ½ cup low-sodium marinara sauce
- 2 tbsp unsweetened almond milk or other plant-based milk
- ½ tsp dried oregano

Directions:
1. Preheat your oven to 220°C (425°F). Line a baking sheet with parchment paper.
2. In a shallow bowl, combine breadcrumbs, nutritional yeast, garlic powder, smoked paprika, black pepper and salt, if using.
3. Place almond milk in a separate shallow bowl.
4. Dip each zucchini stick into almond milk, then roll it in the breadcrumb mixture to coat evenly.
5. Place coated zucchini sticks on the prepared baking sheet in a single layer. Bake for 15-20 minutes, flipping halfway through, until zucchini sticks are golden and crispy.
6. While zucchini sticks are baking, warm marinara sauce in a saucepan over low heat. Stir in dried oregano.
7. Arrange zucchini sticks on a serving plate with warm marinara sauce on the side for dipping.

Nutritional Information (per serving): Calories: 180 kcal; Protein: 6 g; Carbohydrates: 22 g; Fats: 6 g; Fiber: 4 g; Cholesterol: 0 mg; Sodium: 200 mg; Potassium: 500 mg

# Smoky Eggplant Dip with Whole-Grain Crackers

*Prep. time: 10 min | Cook Time: 25 min | Serves: 2*

Ingredients:
- 1 medium eggplant, halved lengthwise
- 1 clove garlic, minced
- 1 tbsp tahini
- 1 tbsp fresh lemon juice
- ½ tsp smoked paprika
- ¼ tsp ground cumin
- 1 tsp olive oil
- ¼ tsp salt (optional)
- ¼ tsp black pepper
- 8-10 whole-grain crackers

Directions:
1. Preheat oven to 200°C (400°F).
2. Place eggplant halves on a baking sheet, cut side down. Roast for 20-25 minutes or until flesh is tender and skin is slightly charred.
3. Once eggplant is cool enough to handle, scoop out the flesh and place it in a food processor or blender.
4. Add garlic, tahini, lemon juice, smoked paprika, cumin, olive oil, salt and black pepper. Blend until creamy.
5. Taste dip and adjust seasoning as needed with additional lemon juice, salt or paprika.
6. Transfer smoky eggplant dip to a serving bowl. Serve with whole-grain crackers for dipping.
7. Pair this dip with fresh vegetable sticks like carrot, cucumber or bell pepper slices for added crunch.

Nutritional Information (per serving): Calories: 180 kcal; Protein: 5 g; Carbohydrates: 22 g; Fats: 8 g; Fiber: 6 g; Cholesterol: 0 mg; Sodium: 150 mg; Potassium: 480 mg

# Herb-Infused Brown Rice Pilaf

*Prep. time: 5 min | Cook time: 30 min | Serves: 2*

Ingredients:
- ½ cup brown rice
- 1 cup low-sodium vegetable broth or water
- ¼ cup diced carrots
- 1 tbsp olive oil
- ¼ cup yellow onion, finely diced
- 1 clove garlic, minced
- 1 tsp fresh thyme leaves
- 1 tsp fresh parsley, chopped (plus more for garnish)
- ¼ tsp ground black pepper
- ¼ tsp salt (optional)

Directions:
1. Rinse brown rice under cold water to remove excess starch.
2. Heat olive oil in a medium saucepan over medium heat. Sauté onion and garlic for 2-3 minutes.
3. Add rinsed brown rice to the saucepan and toast for 2 minutes, stirring frequently, to enhance its flavour.
4. Pour in vegetable broth or water and bring to a boil. Add diced carrots, thyme, black pepper and salt.
5. Reduce heat to low, cover and simmer for 25-30 minutes or until rice is tender and liquid is absorbed.
6. Remove saucepan from heat and fluff rice with a fork. Stir in fresh parsley for added brightness and flavour.
7. Transfer pilaf to a serving dish and garnish with additional parsley. Serve warm.

Nutritional Information (per serving): Calories: 210 kcal; Protein: 4 g; Carbohydrates: 34 g; Fats: 5 g; Fiber: 3 g; Cholesterol: 0 mg; Sodium: 180 mg; Potassium: 250 mg

# Crispy Baked Tofu Nuggets

*Prep. time: 10 min | Cook Time: 25 min | Serves: 2*

Ingredients:
- 1 block (225gm/8oz) firm tofu, cubed
- 2 tbsp unsweetened almond milk or other plant-based milk
- 1 tbsp low-sodium soy sauce or tamari
- ½ cup whole-grain breadcrumbs or gluten-free alternative
- 2 tbsp nutritional yeast
- ½ tsp smoked paprika
- ¼ tsp garlic powder
- ¼ tsp onion powder
- ¼ tsp black pepper
- ¼ tsp salt (optional)

Directions:
1. Preheat oven to 200°C (400°F). Line a baking sheet with parchment paper.
2. Press tofu to remove excess moisture, then cut it into bite-sized cubes.
3. In a small bowl, whisk together almond milk and soy sauce.
4. In another bowl, mix breadcrumbs, nutritional yeast, smoked paprika, garlic powder, onion powder, black pepper and salt, if using.
5. Dip each tofu cube into the almond milk mixture, then roll it in the breadcrumb mixture to coat evenly.
6. Place coated tofu cubes on the prepared baking sheet in a single layer. Bake for 20-25 minutes, flipping halfway through, until tofu nuggets are golden and crispy.
7. Transfer tofu nuggets to a serving plate and serve with warm marinara or tahini dressing for dipping.

Nutritional Information (per serving): Calories: 220 kcal; Protein: 14 g; Carbohydrates: 18 g; Fats: 8 g; Fiber: 3 g; Cholesterol: 0 mg; Sodium: 240 mg; Potassium: 220 mg

# Avocado and Lime Guacamole with Veggie Sticks

*Prep. time: 10 min | Cook time: 0 min | Serves: 2*

Ingredients:
- 1 ripe avocado
- 1 tbsp fresh lime juice
- 1 clove garlic, minced
- 1 tbsp red onion, finely diced
- ¼ tsp black pepper
- ¼ tsp salt (optional)
- 1 tbsp fresh cilantro, chopped
- 1 small carrot, cut into sticks
- 1 small cucumber, cut into sticks
- ½ red bell pepper, cut into strips

Directions:
1. Cut avocado in half, remove pit and scoop flesh into a bowl. Mash avocado with a fork until smooth or leave slightly chunky, depending on your preference.
2. Stir in lime juice, garlic, red onion, black pepper and salt, if using. Mix well, then fold in chopped cilantro.
3. Wash and cut carrot, cucumber and bell pepper into sticks or strips for dipping.
4. Transfer guacamole to a serving bowl and arrange vegetables on a plate alongside it. Serve immediately.
   *Can be enjoyed as a healthy snack or light appetizer.

Nutritional Information (per serving): Calories: 180 kcal; Protein: 3 g; Carbohydrates: 15 g; Fats: 14 g; Fiber: 7 g; Cholesterol: 0 mg; Sodium: 80 mg; Potassium: 450 mg

# Spicy Roasted Chickpeas

*Prep. time: 5 min | Cook Time: 25 min | Serves: 2*

Ingredients:
- 1 cup low sodium canned chickpeas, rinsed and drained
- 1 tbsp olive oil
- ½ tsp smoked paprika
- ½ tsp ground cumin
- ¼ tsp cayenne pepper
- ¼ tsp garlic powder
- ¼ tsp black pepper
- ¼ tsp salt (optional)

Directions:
1. Preheat oven to 200°C (400°F). Line a baking sheet with parchment paper.
2. Spread rinsed and drained chickpeas on a clean paper towel. Pat dry thoroughly to ensure crispiness.
3. In a mixing bowl, toss chickpeas with olive oil, smoked paprika, cumin, cayenne pepper, garlic powder, black pepper and salt, if using. Spread seasoned chickpeas in a single layer on the prepared baking sheet.
4. Roast for 20-25 minutes, stirring halfway through, until they are golden and crispy.
5. Let chickpeas cool slightly before serving, as they will continue to crisp up as they cool.

   *Serve these spicy roasted chickpeas as a snack, salad topping or a crunchy addition to soups.

Nutritional Information (per serving): Calories: 180 kcal; Protein: 6 g; Carbohydrates: 20 g; Fats: 6 g; Fiber: 5 g; Cholesterol: 0 mg; Sodium: 150 mg; Potassium: 220 mg

# Baked Falafel Bites with Cucumber Yogurt Sauce

*Prep. time: 15 min | Cook time: 20 min | Serves: 2*

Ingredients:
- 1 cup low-sodium canned chickpeas, rinsed and drained
- ¼ cup fresh parsley, chopped
- 1 clove garlic, minced
- 2 tbsp whole-grain breadcrumbs or gluten-free alternative
- 1 tbsp olive oil (plus extra for greasing)
- ½ tsp ground cumin
- ¼ tsp smoked paprika
- ¼ tsp salt (optional)
- ¼ tsp black pepper
- ¼ cup plain unsweetened plant-based yogurt
- ¼ cup cucumber, grated and drained
- 1 tsp fresh lemon juice

Directions:
1. Preheat oven to 190°C (375°F). Lightly grease a baking sheet with olive oil.
2. In a food processor, combine chickpeas, parsley, garlic, breadcrumbs, olive oil, cumin, smoked paprika, black pepper and salt, if using. Pulse until mixture is well combined but not completely smooth.
3. Form mixture into small bite-sized balls or patties. Place them evenly on the prepared baking sheet.
4. Bake for 20 minutes, flipping halfway through, until golden and crispy on the outside.
5. In a small bowl, mix yogurt, grated cucumber and lemon juice until well combined. Adjust seasoning to taste.
6. Serve falafel bites with cucumber yogurt sauce on the side for dipping.

Nutritional Information (per serving): Calories: 200 kcal; Protein: 7 g; Carbohydrates: 22 g; Fats: 7 g; Fiber: 5 g; Cholesterol: 0 mg; Sodium: 150 mg; Potassium: 250 mg

# Sesame Green Beans with Soy Glaze

*Prep. time: 5 min | Cook Time: 10 min | Serves: 2*

Ingredients:
- 2 cups fresh green beans, trimmed
- 1 tbsp low-sodium soy sauce
- 1 tsp sesame oil
- 1 clove garlic, minced
- ½ tsp fresh ginger, grated
- 1 tsp rice vinegar
- ½ tsp maple syrup or honey
- 1 tsp sesame seeds (plus more for garnish)

Directions:
1. Bring a pot of water to a boil.
2. Add green beans and blanch for 2-3 minutes until tender crisp. Drain and immediately transfer to a bowl of ice water to stop the cooking process. Drain again and set aside.
3. In a small bowl, whisk together soy sauce, sesame oil, garlic, ginger, rice vinegar, maple syrup and 1 tbsp of water.
4. Heat a non-stick skillet over medium heat. Add prepared green beans and soy glaze mixture. Toss to coat.
5. Cook for 3-4 minutes, stirring frequently, until glaze thickens slightly, and green beans are heated through.
6. Sprinkle sesame seeds over the green beans and toss again to combine.
7. Transfer green beans to a serving dish and garnish with additional sesame seeds. Serve warm.

Nutritional Information (per serving): Calories: 90 kcal; Protein: 3 g; Carbohydrates: 8 g; Fats: 4 g; Fiber: 2 g; Cholesterol: 0 mg; Sodium: 170 mg; Potassium: 250 mg

# Broccoli Slaw with Sesame Dressing

*Prep. time: 10 min | Cook time: 0 min | Serves: 2*

Ingredients:
- 2 cups broccoli stems, shredded
- ½ cup carrot, shredded
- ¼ cup red cabbage, thinly sliced
- 1 tbsp sesame seeds (plus extra for garnish)
- 1 tbsp tahini
- 1 tbsp low-sodium soy sauce or tamari
- 1 tsp sesame oil
- 1 tbsp rice vinegar
- ½ tsp maple syrup or honey
- ¼ tsp fresh ginger, grated

Directions:
1. Wash broccoli stems, carrots and red cabbage thoroughly. Shred broccoli stems and carrots using a box grater or food processor. Thinly slice red cabbage into strips.
2. In a large mixing bowl, combine shredded broccoli stems, carrot, red cabbage and sesame seeds.
3. In a small bowl, whisk together tahini, soy sauce, sesame oil, rice vinegar, maple syrup and grated ginger.
4. Pour sesame dressing over the vegetable mixture. Toss to coat evenly.
5. Transfer broccoli slaw to a serving bowl and garnish with additional sesame seeds. Serve immediately or let chill in the refrigerator for 15 minutes to enhance flavours.

   *Serve this slaw as a side dish to grilled tofu or baked salmon, or as a filling in whole-grain wraps.

Nutritional Information (per serving): Calories: 130 kcal; Protein: 4 g; Carbohydrates: 10 g; Fats: 9 g; Fiber: 3 g; Cholesterol: 0 mg; Sodium: 160 mg; Potassium: 300 mg

# Hearty Lentil and Veggie Pâté

*Prep. time: 10 min | Cook Time: 20 min | Serves: 2*

Ingredients:
- 1 cup cooked green or brown lentils
- ½ cup mushrooms, finely chopped
- ¼ cup onion, finely diced
- 1 clove garlic, minced
- 1 tbsp olive oil
- 1 tbsp fresh parsley, chopped
- ½ tsp smoked paprika
- ¼ tsp dried thyme
- ¼ tsp black pepper
- ¼ tsp salt
- A pinch of smoked paprika

Directions:
1. Heat olive oil in a skillet over medium heat. Add onions, garlic and mushrooms. Cook for 5-7 minutes until softened and fragrant.
2. In a food processor, combine cooked lentils, sautéed vegetables, parsley, smoked paprika, thyme, black pepper and salt.
3. Pulse mixture until smooth but slightly textured, scraping down the sides as needed.
4. Transfer mixture to a serving bowl. Cover and refrigerate for at least 15 minutes to allow flavours to meld.
5. Garnish with additional parsley and a sprinkle of smoked paprika. Serve with whole-grain crackers, vegetable sticks or as a spread on whole-grain bread.

Nutritional Information (per serving): Calories: 180 kcal; Protein: 8 g; Carbohydrates: 18 g; Fats: 7 g; Fiber: 6 g; Cholesterol: 0 mg; Sodium: 120 mg; Potassium: 450 mg

# Smashed Baby Potatoes with Garlic and Chives

*Prep. time: 10 min | Cook time: 30 min | Serves: 2*

Ingredients:
- 10 small baby potatoes
- 1 tbsp olive oil
- 1 clove garlic, minced
- ¼ tsp smoked paprika
- ¼ tsp black pepper
- ¼ tsp salt (optional)
- 1 tbsp fresh chives, chopped (for garnish)

Directions:
1. Bring a pot of water to a boil.
   Add baby potatoes and cook for 15-20 minutes, until fork tender.
   Drain and let cool slightly.
2. Preheat oven to 220°C (425°F). Line a baking sheet with parchment paper.
3. Place boiled potatoes on the baking sheet. Using a fork or the bottom of a glass, gently press each potato to flatten it slightly while keeping it intact.
4. Drizzle olive oil over smashed potatoes. Sprinkle with garlic, smoked paprika, black pepper and salt, if using.
5. Roast in the oven for 15-20 minutes or until edges are crispy and golden.
6. Remove potatoes from the oven and sprinkle with fresh chives. Serve warm.

Nutritional Information (per serving): Calories: 180 kcal; Protein: 3 g; Carbohydrates: 28 g; Fats: 5 g; Fiber: 3 g; Cholesterol: 0 mg; Sodium: 150 mg; Potassium: 450 mg

# Cauliflower Mash with Fresh Thyme

*Prep. time: 5 min | Cook Time: 10 min | Serves: 2*

Ingredients:
- 1 medium head cauliflower, chopped (approx. 3 cups florets)
- 1 clove garlic, minced
- 1 tbsp olive oil
- ¼ cup unsweetened almond milk or other plant-based milk
- 1 tsp fresh thyme leaves
- ¼ tsp black pepper
- ¼ tsp salt (optional)
- A sprinkle of smoked paprika

Directions:
1. Bring a pot of water to a boil. Add cauliflower florets and cook for 10-12 minutes or until very tender. Drain well.
2. In a blender or food processor, combine cooked cauliflower, garlic, olive oil, almond milk, fresh thyme, black pepper and salt, if using.
3. Blend mixture until creamy and smooth, stopping to scrape down the sides as needed.
4. Taste mash and adjust seasoning with additional salt, pepper or thyme, if desired.
5. Transfer cauliflower mash to a serving dish. Garnish with smoked paprika and fresh thyme and serve warm.

*Pair this creamy cauliflower mash with baked tofu or grilled salmon for a balanced, heart-healthy meal.

Nutritional Information (per serving): Calories: 110 kcal; Protein: 3 g; Carbohydrates: 9 g; Fats: 7 g; Fiber: 3 g; Cholesterol: 0 mg; Sodium: 120 mg; Potassium: 350 mg

# Sweet Corn Salad with Lime and Cilantro

*Prep. time: 10 min | Cook time: 5 min | Serves: 2*

Ingredients:
- 1 cup fresh or frozen sweet corn kernels
- ¼ cup red bell pepper, finely diced
- ¼ cup red onion, finely diced
- 1 tbsp fresh cilantro, chopped
- 1 tbsp fresh lime juice
- 1 tsp olive oil
- ¼ tsp ground cumin
- ¼ tsp black pepper
- ¼ tsp salt (optional)
- 1 tbsp diced avocado (optional)
- 1 tbsp crumbled feta cheese (if not strictly cholesterol-free)

Directions:
1. If using fresh corn, boil the kernels in water for 3-4 minutes or until tender. Drain and let cool. If using frozen corn, thaw according to package instructions and pat dry.
2. In a large mixing bowl, combine cooked corn, red bell pepper, red onion and cilantro.
3. In a small bowl, whisk together lime juice, olive oil, cumin, black pepper and salt, if using.
4. Pour dressing over the corn mixture. Toss until everything is evenly coated.
5. Transfer salad to a serving dish and garnish with cilantro or optional toppings like avocado or crumbled feta.

*Serve as a light side dish with grilled vegetables, roasted tofu or as a topping for tacos or wraps.

Nutritional Information (per serving): Calories: 110 kcal; Protein: 2 g; Carbohydrates: 16 g; Fats: 4 g; Fiber: 2 g; Cholesterol: 0 mg; Sodium: 60 mg; Potassium: 220 mg

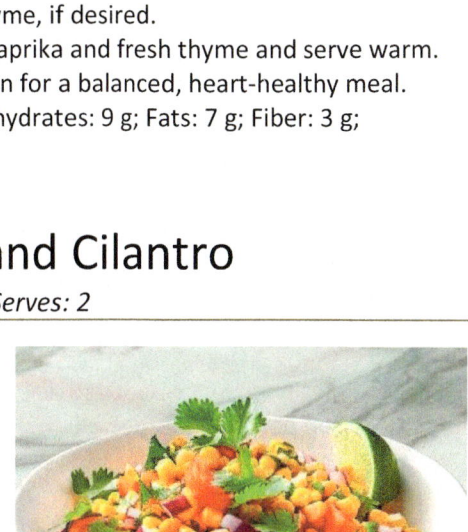

# Roasted Carrot and Parsnip Medley

*Prep. time: 10 min | Cook time: 25 min | Serves: 2*

Ingredients:
- 2 medium carrots, peeled and cut into sticks
- 2 medium parsnips, peeled and cut into sticks
- 1 tbsp olive oil
- 1 tsp maple syrup
- ½ tsp smoked paprika
- ½ tsp garlic powder
- ¼ tsp black pepper
- ¼ tsp salt (optional)
- 1 tsp fresh parsley, chopped (for garnish)

Directions:
1. Preheat oven to 200°C (400°F). Line a baking sheet with parchment paper.
2. Peel carrots and parsnips, then cut them into evenly sized sticks.
3. Place carrot and parsnip sticks in a large mixing bowl. Drizzle olive oil and maple syrup over the vegetables. Add smoked paprika, garlic powder, black pepper and salt, if using. Toss to coat evenly.
4. Spread seasoned vegetables in a single layer on the prepared baking sheet. Roast for 20-25 minutes, stirring halfway through, until carrots and parsnips are tender and slightly caramelized.
5. Transfer roasted vegetables to a serving plate. Garnish with fresh parsley before serving.

Nutritional Information (per serving): Calories: 150 kcal; Protein: 2 g; Carbohydrates: 21 g; Fats: 7 g; Fiber: 5 g; Cholesterol: 0 mg; Sodium: 120 mg; Potassium: 450 mg

# Balsamic Glazed Roasted Pearl (baby) Onions

*Prep. time: 10 min | Cook Time: 25 min | Serves: 2*

Ingredients:
- 1 cup pearl onions, peeled
- 1 tbsp olive oil
- 2 tbsp balsamic vinegar
- 1 tsp maple syrup
- ½ tsp fresh thyme leaves
- ¼ tsp black pepper
- Pinch of salt

Directions:
1. Preheat oven to 200°C (400°F).
2. If pearl onions are not pre-peeled, blanch them in boiling water for 1-2 minutes, drain and peel off the skins.
3. In a mixing bowl, toss onions with olive oil, balsamic vinegar, maple syrup, thyme, black pepper and salt.
4. Spread seasoned onions in a single layer on a baking sheet lined with parchment paper. Roast in the oven for 20-25 minutes, stirring halfway through, until onions are tender and caramelized.
5. Remove onions from the oven and toss them in the glaze on the baking sheet to coat evenly.
6. Transfer roasted pearl onions to a serving dish. Garnish with additional fresh thyme, if desired and serve warm.

   *Can be served as a side dish for baked salmon or as a topping for whole-grain salads or flatbreads.

Nutritional Information (per serving): Calories: 120 kcal; Protein: 1 g; Carbohydrates: 14 g; Fats: 7 g; Fiber: 2 g; Cholesterol: 0 mg; Sodium: 50 mg; Potassium: 180 mg

# Roasted Bell Pepper Hummus with Pita Wedges

*Prep. time: 10 min | Cook Time: 25 min | Serves: 2*

Ingredients:
- 1 medium red bell pepper
- 1 low-sodium cup canned chickpeas, rinsed and drained
- 1 tbsp tahini
- 1 clove garlic, minced
- 1 tbsp fresh lemon juice
- ½ tsp ground cumin
- ¼ tsp smoked paprika
- ¼ tsp salt (optional)
- 2 tbsp olive oil, divided
- 2 whole-grain pita breads

Directions:
1. Preheat oven to 220°C (425°F). Place red bell pepper on a baking sheet and roast for 20 minutes, turning halfway through, until skin is charred and blistered.
2. Remove bell pepper from the oven, place it in a bowl and cover with plastic wrap for 5 minutes to loosen skin. Peel off skin, remove seeds and chop into pieces.
3. In a food processor, combine roasted bell pepper, chickpeas, tahini, garlic, lemon juice, cumin, smoked paprika and salt, if using. Blend until smooth. Slowly add 1 tbsp of olive oil for a creamy consistency.
4. While bell pepper is roasting, cut pita breads into wedges and brush them with the remaining olive oil.
5. Place wedges on a baking sheet and bake for 5-7 minutes at 190°C (375°F) until crisp and lightly golden.
6. Transfer hummus to a serving bowl. Garnish with a sprinkle of smoked paprika and fresh parsley. Serve with warm pita wedges.

Nutritional Information (per serving): Calories: 230 kcal; Protein: 7 g; Carbohydrates: 26 g; Fats: 10 g; Fiber: 6 g; Cholesterol: 0 mg; Sodium: 150 mg; Potassium: 280 mg

# Coconut-Lime Cauliflower Rice

*Prep. time: 5 min | Cook time: 10 min | Serves: 2*

Ingredients:
- 2 cups cauliflower rice, fresh or frozen
- ¼ cup light coconut milk
- 1 tsp coconut oil
- 1 clove garlic, minced
- 1 tsp fresh lime zest
- 1 tbsp fresh lime juice
- ¼ tsp ground cumin
- Pinch of salt
- 1 tbsp fresh cilantro, chopped (for garnish)

Directions:
1. If using fresh cauliflower, pulse florets in a food processor or grate them using a box grater until they resemble rice grains. If using frozen cauliflower rice, thaw it beforehand.
2. Heat coconut oil in a large skillet over medium heat. Add minced garlic and sauté for 1 minute until fragrant.
3. Add cauliflower rice to the skillet. Cook for 5-6 minutes, stirring occasionally, until softened.
4. Stir in light coconut milk, lime zest, lime juice, ground cumin and salt. Cook for an additional 2-3 minutes.
5. Remove from the heat and transfer to a serving dish. Garnish with fresh cilantro and a sprinkle of lime zest.

Nutritional Information (per serving): Calories: 90 kcal; Protein: 2 g; Carbohydrates: 8 g; Fats: 5 g; Fiber: 3 g; Cholesterol: 0 mg; Sodium: 70 mg; Potassium: 240 mg

# Cholesterol-Conscious Dessert Delights

# Coconut Milk Rice Pudding with Mango

*Prep. time: 5 min | Cook Time: 25 min | Serves: 2*

Ingredients:
- ½ cup jasmine or basmati rice
- 1 cup light coconut milk
- ½ cup water
- ¼ tsp ground cardamom
- 2 tbsp maple syrup or coconut sugar
- ½ tsp vanilla extract
- ½ cup fresh mango, diced
- 1 tsp shredded coconut (for garnish)

Directions:
1. Rinse rice under cold water until water runs clear.
2. In a medium saucepan, combine rice, coconut milk, water and ground cardamom. Bring to a gentle boil over medium heat.
3. Reduce heat to low and cover saucepan. Simmer for 20 minutes, stirring occasionally to prevent sticking, until rice is tender, and mixture has thickened.
4. Stir in maple syrup and vanilla extract. Cook for an additional 2-3 minutes, stirring to combine.
5. Remove saucepan from the heat and let pudding cool slightly.
6. Divide rice pudding into two bowls, top with diced mango and shredded coconut. Serve warm or chilled.

Nutritional Information (per serving): Calories: 210 kcal; Protein: 3 g; Carbohydrates: 35 g; Fats: 6 g; Fiber: 2 g; Cholesterol: 0 mg; Sodium: 30 mg; Potassium: 150 mg

# Baked Cinnamon Pears with Walnuts

*Prep. time: 5 min | Cook time: 20 min | Serves: 2*

Ingredients:
- 2 medium pears, halved and cored
- 2 tbsp walnuts, chopped
- 1 tbsp maple syrup
- ½ tsp ground cinnamon
- ¼ tsp ground nutmeg
- ½ tsp vanilla extract
- 1 tbsp water
- 1 tsp unsweetened shredded coconut (optional)
- 1 tbsp plant-based yogurt (optional)

Directions:
1. Preheat oven to 190°C (375°F).
   Line a baking dish with parchment paper.
2. Place pear halves cut-side up in the baking dish.
3. In a small bowl, mix walnuts, maple syrup, cinnamon, nutmeg and vanilla extract. Spoon this mixture evenly into the hollowed-out cores of the pears.
4. Add 1 tbsp of water to the baking dish to prevent pears from drying out.
5. Bake in the preheated oven for 20 minutes or until pears are tender and golden.
6. Remove pears from the oven and let them cool slightly. Transfer to serving plates and garnish with shredded coconut or a dollop of plant-based yogurt, if desired. Serve warm.

   *Enjoy as a dessert with a side of herbal tea or sprinkle with granola for a light breakfast option

Nutritional Information (per serving): Calories: 150 kcal; Protein: 2 g; Carbohydrates: 24 g; Fats: 6 g; Fiber: 4 g; Cholesterol: 0 mg; Sodium: 5 mg; Potassium: 210 mg

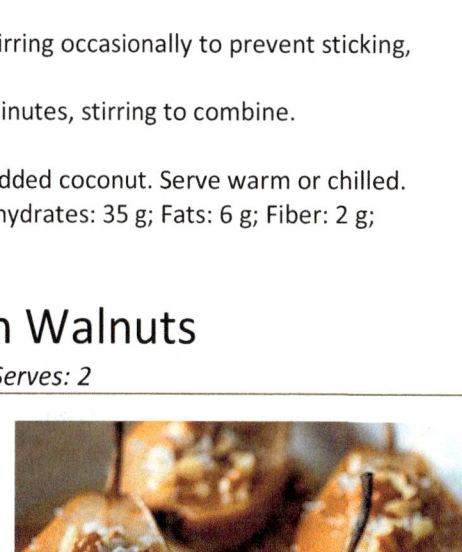

# Avocado Chocolate Mousse

*Prep. time: 10 min | Cook Time: 0 minutes | Serves: 2*

Ingredients:
- 1 large ripe avocado, peeled and pitted
- 2 tbsp unsweetened cacao powder
- 2 tbsp maple syrup or agave nectar (adjust to taste)
- ¼ cup unsweetened almond milk or any plant-based milk
- 1 tsp vanilla extract
- ¼ tsp ground cinnamon
- Pinch of sea salt
- Fresh berries (for garnish)
- Dairy-free dark chocolate, shaved (for garnish)
- Crushed nuts (almonds or hazelnuts, for garnish)

Directions:
1. Scoop avocado into a food processor or blender.
   Add cocoa powder, maple syrup, almond milk, vanilla extract, cinnamon and sea salt. Blend until smooth and creamy, scraping down the sides as needed.
2. Taste mousse and adjust sweetness by adding more maple syrup, if desired. If mousse is too thick, add a little more almond milk, 1 tsp at a time, until it reaches your desired consistency.
3. Divide mousse into two serving bowls. Refrigerate for at least 30 minutes to allow the texture to firm up.
4. Top with fresh berries, shaved dark chocolate or crushed nuts before serving. Enjoy chilled.

Nutritional Information (per serving): Calories: 210 kcal; Protein: 3 g; Carbohydrates: 19 g; Fats: 15 g; Fiber: 6 g; Cholesterol: 0 mg; Sodium: 40 mg; Potassium: 380 mg

# Vegan Apple Crumble with Oats

*Prep. time: 10 min | Cook time: 25 min | Serves: 2*

Ingredients:
- 2 medium apples, peeled, cored and chopped
- 1 tbsp maple syrup (adjust to taste)
- ½ tsp ground cinnamon
- ¼ tsp ground nutmeg
- 1 tsp fresh lemon juice
- ¼ cup rolled oats
- 2 tbsp almond flour or whole-wheat flour
- 1 tbsp chopped walnuts
- 1 tbsp coconut oil, melted
- 1 tbsp maple syrup

Directions:
1. Preheat oven to 190°C (375°F). Lightly grease two small ramekins or an oven-safe dish.
2. In a mixing bowl, combine apple pieces, maple syrup, cinnamon, nutmeg and lemon juice. Toss until apples are evenly coated. Divide apple mixture evenly between the ramekins.
3. In another bowl, mix rolled oats, almond flour, chopped walnuts, coconut oil and maple syrup. Stir until mixture is crumbly and well combined.
4. Spoon crumble topping evenly over the apple filling in each ramekin. Place ramekins on a baking sheet and bake for 25 minutes or until apples are tender and topping is golden brown.
5. Remove from the oven and let cool slightly. Serve warm on its own or with a dollop of plant-based yogurt.

Nutritional Information (per serving): Calories: 180 kcal; Protein: 3 g; Carbohydrates: 30 g; Fats: 7 g; Fiber: 4 g; Cholesterol: 0 mg; Sodium: 15 mg; Potassium: 200 mg

# Sweet Potato Brownies with Cacao

*Prep. time: 10 min | Cook time: 25 min | Serves: 2*

Ingredients:
- 1 small, sweet potato, peeled and diced
- 2 tbsp unsweetened cacao powder
- 2 tbsp almond flour
- 1 tbsp maple syrup (adjust to taste)
- 1 tbsp almond butter
- ½ tsp vanilla extract
- ¼ tsp baking powder
- Pinch of salt
- 1 tbsp dairy-free dark chocolate chips (optional)
- 1 tbsp chopped walnuts (optional)

Directions:
1. Preheat oven to 175°C (350°F). Line small baking dish or loaf pan with parchment paper.
2. Cook sweet potato by steaming or microwaving until soft. Peel and mash thoroughly to remove lumps, ensuring it produces ½ cup mashed sweet potato.
3. In a mixing bowl, combine mashed sweet potato, cacao powder, almond flour, maple syrup, almond butter, vanilla extract, baking powder and salt. Mix until a smooth batter forms.
4. If using, fold in dark chocolate chips or chopped walnuts.
5. Pour batter into the prepared baking dish, spreading it evenly. Bake for 20-25 minutes or until toothpick inserted into the center comes out clean.
6. Let brownies cool in the pan for 10 minutes, then transfer to a wire rack to cool completely. Slice and serve.

Nutritional Information (per serving): Calories: 150 kcal; Protein: 4 g; Carbohydrates: 20 g; Fats: 6 g; Fiber: 4 g; Cholesterol: 0 mg; Sodium: 60 mg; Potassium: 200 mg

# Chocolate-Covered Dates with Almond Butter Filling

*Prep. time: 15 min | Setting Time: 20 min | Serves: 2 (makes 6 stuffed dates)*

Ingredients:
- 6 Medjool dates, pitted
- 2 tbsp unsweetened almond butter, smooth or chunky
- ¼ cup dairy-free dark chocolate chips
- ½ tsp coconut oil
- 1 tbsp crushed almonds
- ¼ tsp sea salt (for garnish)

Directions:
1. Slice each Medjool date lengthwise to create an opening, but do not cut all the way through. Remove pits if not pitted.
2. Using a small spoon, fill each date with about 1 tsp of almond butter. Press date closed gently to secure the filling.
3. In a microwave-safe bowl, combine dark chocolate chips and coconut oil. Microwave in 15-second intervals, stirring between each, until fully melted and smooth.
4. Using a fork or skewer, dip each almond butter-filled date into the melted chocolate, ensuring it is fully coated. Place dipped dates on a parchment-lined plate or tray.
5. Sprinkle each date with crushed almonds and a tiny pinch of sea salt, before chocolate hardens.
6. Refrigerate chocolate-covered dates for 15-20 minutes or until chocolate is firm.

Nutritional Information (per serving): Calories: 180 kcal; Protein: 3 g; Carbohydrates: 25 g; Fats: 9 g; Fiber: 4 g; Cholesterol: 0 mg; Sodium: 50 mg; Potassium: 240 mg

# Sugar-Free Lemon Coconut Bars

*Prep. time: 10 min | Setting Time: 1 hour (refrigeration) | Serves: 2*

Ingredients:
- ¼ cup almond flour
- 1 tbsp coconut flour
- 1 tbsp unsweetened shredded coconut
- 1 tbsp coconut oil, melted
- 2 tbsp maple syrup, divided
- ¼ cup fresh lemon juice
- 1 tsp lemon zest
- ¼ cup coconut cream
  (scooped from the top of a chilled coconut milk can)
- 1 tsp arrowroot powder or cornstarch
- Extra shredded coconut or lemon zest (for garnish)

Directions:
1. In a small mixing bowl, combine almond flour, coconut flour, shredded coconut, melted coconut oil and 1 tbsp of maple syrup. Mix until the mixture holds together when pressed.
2. Press mixture evenly into a small parchment paper lined container. Refrigerate while preparing lemon filling.
3. In a small saucepan, combine lemon juice, lemon zest, coconut cream and 1 tbsp of maple syrup. Cook over medium heat, stirring frequently, until warmed through.
4. In a separate small bowl, dissolve arrowroot powder or cornstarch in 1 tbsp of water. Slowly whisk this mixture into the saucepan. Cook for 2-3 minutes, stirring constantly, until mixture thickens.
5. Pour lemon filling over the chilled base and spread it evenly. Sprinkle with shredded coconut or lemon zest.
6. Refrigerate assembled bars for at least 1 hour or until fully set.
7. Once set, lift bars out using parchment paper and slice into squares. Serve chilled.

Nutritional Information (per serving): Calories: 180 kcal; Protein: 3 g; Carbohydrates: 9 g; Fats: 14 g; Fiber: 3 g; Cholesterol: 0 mg; Sodium: 20 mg; Potassium: 90 mg

# Mango and Passionfruit Sorbet

*Prep. time: 10 min | Freezing Time: 2-3 hours | Serves: 2*

Ingredients:
- 1 cup fresh or frozen mango, diced
- 2 passionfruit, pulp only
- 2 tbsp fresh orange juice
- 1 tbsp maple syrup or liquid stevia (adjust to taste)
- ½ tsp fresh lime zest

Directions:
1. If using fresh mango, dice it and freeze for at least 2-3 hours or until fully frozen.
2. In a blender or food processor, combine frozen mango, passionfruit pulp, orange juice, maple syrup and lime zest. Blend until smooth and creamy, stopping to scrape down the sides as needed.
3. Taste mixture and add more maple syrup, if a sweeter flavour is desired. Blend again briefly to combine.
4. Transfer blended mixture to an airtight container and freeze for 1-2 hours for a firmer consistency or serve immediately for a soft-serve texture.
5. Scoop sorbet into bowls and garnish with additional passionfruit pulp or a sprinkle of lime zest.

Nutritional Information (per serving): Calories: 80 kcal; Protein: 1 g; Carbohydrates: 20 g; Fats: 0 g; Fiber: 2 g; Cholesterol: 0 mg; Sodium: 5 mg; Potassium: 170 mg

# Vegan Blueberry Almond Tart

*Prep. time: 15 min | Cook Time: 20 min | Serves: 2*

Ingredients:
- ¼ cup almond flour
- 2 tbsp rolled oats
- 1 tbsp coconut oil, melted
- 2 tbsp maple syrup, divided
- ½ cup fresh or frozen blueberries
- 2 tbsp unsweetened almond milk
- 1 tsp cornstarch or arrowroot powder
- ¼ tsp almond extract
- 1 tbsp slivered almonds, toasted (for garnish)
- ½ tsp lemon zest (for garnish)

Directions:
1. Preheat oven to 175°C (350°F). Lightly grease two small tart pans or ramekins with coconut oil.
2. In a small bowl, mix almond flour, rolled oats, coconut oil and 1 tbsp of maple syrup until it holds together.
3. Press mixture evenly into tart pans and bake for 8-10 minutes until golden. Remove from oven and let cool.
4. In a small saucepan, combine blueberries, almond milk and 1 tbsp of maple syrup. Cook over medium heat, stirring occasionally, until blueberries begin to break down, about 5 minutes.
5. Dissolve cornstarch or arrowroot powder in 1 tsp of water. Stir this mixture into the blueberry mixture and cook for another 1-2 minutes until thickened. Remove from heat and stir in almond extract.
6. Spoon blueberry filling into the prepared tart crusts and bake in the oven for an additional 8-10 minutes.
7. Let tarts cool slightly before removing from the pans, garnish with almonds and lemon zest and serve.

Nutritional Information (per serving): Calories: 180 kcal; Protein: 4 g; Carbohydrates: 18 g; Fats: 10 g; Fiber: 3 g; Cholesterol: 0 mg; Sodium: 15 mg; Potassium: 110 mg

# Almond and Date Energy Bars

*Prep. time: 10 min | Setting Time: 1 hours (refrigeration) | Serves: 2*

Ingredients:
- 6 Medjool dates, pitted
- ¼ cup almonds, raw or lightly toasted
- 2 tbsp rolled oats
- 1 tbsp almond butter
- 1 tbsp chia seeds or flaxseeds
- 1 tbsp unsweetened shredded coconut
- ¼ tsp ground cinnamon
- ½ tsp vanilla extract
- 1 tbsp dark chocolate chips or cacao nibs

Directions:
1. If dates are not soft, soak them in warm water for 5-10 minutes, then drain.
2. In a food processor, combine dates, almonds, rolled oats, almond butter, chia seeds, shredded coconut, cinnamon and vanilla extract. Blend into sticky dough, adding water, 1 tsp at a time, if mixture is too dry.
3. Transfer mixture onto a piece of parchment paper. Flatten and shape it into a rectangle about ½ inch thick.
4. Refrigerate the rectangle for 1 hour to firm up.
5. Once chilled, cut the rectangle into 4 bars. Store in an airtight container in the refrigerator for up to 1 week.

Nutritional Information (per serving): Calories: 190 kcal; Protein: 4 g; Carbohydrates: 22 g; Fats: 9 g; Fiber: 4 g; Cholesterol: 0 mg; Sodium: 10 mg; Potassium: 200 mg

# Apricot and Quinoa Cookies

*Prep. time: 10 min | Cook Time: 15 min | Serves: 2*

Ingredients:
- ¼ cup cooked quinoa, cooled
- ¼ cup dried apricots, finely chopped
- 2 tbsp rolled oats
- 2 tbsp almond flour
- 1 tbsp almond butter
- 1 tbsp maple syrup
- ½ tsp vanilla extract
- ¼ tsp ground cinnamon
- ¼ tsp baking powder
- ½ tbsp unsweetened shredded coconut

Directions:
1. Preheat oven to 175°C (350°F). Line a baking sheet with parchment paper.
2. In a medium mixing bowl, combine quinoa, chopped dried apricots, rolled oats, almond flour, almond butter, maple syrup, vanilla extract, cinnamon, baking powder and shredded coconut. Mix until well combined into a sticky dough.
3. Scoop small portions of the dough, about 1 tbsp each, and roll into balls. Flatten gently with your fingers to form cookie shapes and place them on the prepared baking sheet.
4. Bake in the preheated oven for 12-15 minutes or until edges are golden brown.
5. Let cookies cool on the baking sheet for 5 minutes, then transfer to a wire rack to cool completely.

Nutritional Information (per serving): Calories: 150 kcal; Protein: 4 g; Carbohydrates: 20 g; Fats: 6 g; Fiber: 3 g; Cholesterol: 0 mg; Sodium: 10 mg; Potassium: 150 mg

# Roasted Cherry and Almond Crisp

*Prep. time: 10 min | Cook Time: 25 min | Serves: 2*

Ingredients:
- 1 cup fresh or frozen cherries, pitted and halved
- 1 tbsp maple syrup or agave syrup
- ½ tsp ground cinnamon
- ¼ tsp almond extract
- 2 tbsp rolled oats
- 2 tbsp almond flour
- 1 tbsp sliced almonds
- 1 tbsp coconut oil, melted
- 1 tsp maple syrup
- ¼ tsp vanilla extract

Directions:
1. Preheat oven to 175°C (350°F). Lightly grease two small ramekins or an 8-inch baking dish.
2. If using frozen cherries, thaw and drain any excess liquid. In a small bowl, toss cherries with 1 tbsp of maple syrup, cinnamon and almond extract. Divide mixture between ramekins or spread evenly in the baking dish.
3. In another bowl, mix rolled oats, almond flour, sliced almonds, melted coconut oil, 1 tsp of maple syrup and vanilla extract until crumbly. Sprinkle topping mixture evenly over the cherries.
4. Bake in the preheated oven for 20-25 minutes, or until topping is golden brown and cherries are bubbling.
5. Allow crisp to cool slightly before serving.

Nutritional Information (per serving): Calories: 200 kcal; Protein: 4 g; Carbohydrates: 24 g; Fats: 9 g; Fiber: 3 g; Cholesterol: 0 mg; Sodium: 5 mg; Potassium: 230 mg

# Vegan Chocolate Banana Bread

*Prep. time: 10 min | Cook Time: 35 min | Serves: 2*

Ingredients:
- ½ cup whole wheat pastry flour or all-purpose flour
- 1 tbsp unsweetened cacao powder
- ¼ tsp baking soda
- ¼ tsp baking powder
- 1 medium ripe banana, mashed
- 2 tbsp unsweetened almond milk or any plant-based milk
- 2 tbsp maple syrup
- 1 tbsp coconut oil, melted
- ¼ tsp vanilla extract
- 2 tbsp dairy-free dark chocolate chips
- 1 tbsp chopped walnuts

Directions:
1. Preheat oven to 175°C (350°F). Lightly grease a small loaf pan or line it with parchment paper.
2. In a medium bowl, whisk together flour, cocoa powder, baking soda and baking powder.
3. In another bowl, mash banana. Mix it with almond milk, maple syrup, coconut oil and vanilla extract.
4. Pour the wet ingredients into the dry ingredients. Mix gently until just combined; do not overmix.
5. Fold in dark chocolate chips and walnuts.
6. Pour batter into the prepared loaf pan, smoothing top with a spatula. Bake for 30-35 minutes or until a toothpick inserted into the center comes out clean.
7. Cool banana bread in the pan for 5 minutes, then transfer to a wire rack to cool completely before slicing.

Nutritional Information (per serving): Calories: 180 kcal; Protein: 3 g; Carbohydrates: 27 g; Fats: 6 g; Fiber: 3 g; Cholesterol: 0 mg; Sodium: 70 mg; Potassium: 150 mg

# Sesame and Coconut Mochi Bites

*Prep. time: 10 min | Cook Time: 15 min | Serves: 2 (approx. 10 small bites)*

Ingredients:
- ½ cup glutinous rice flour (mochiko)
- ¼ cup unsweetened coconut milk
- 1 tbsp maple syrup or agave syrup
- 1 tbsp sesame seeds, finely ground
- 1 tbsp unsweetened shredded coconut
- ¼ tsp vanilla extract
- ¼ tsp baking powder

Directions:
1. Preheat oven to 175°C (350°F). Lightly grease a mini muffin tin or line it with parchment paper.
2. In a medium mixing bowl, combine glutinous rice flour, ground sesame seeds, baking powder and shredded coconut.
3. In a separate bowl, whisk together coconut milk, maple syrup and vanilla extract.
4. Gradually mix wet ingredients into dry until a thick batter forms, adding water 1 tbsp at a time, if needed.
5. Spoon batter evenly into the prepared mini muffin tin, filling each about ¾ full.
6. Bake in the preheated oven for 12-15 minutes or until mochi bites are slightly puffed and firm to the touch.
7. Allow mochi bites to cool in the tin for 5 minutes before transferring to a wire rack to cool completely.

Nutritional Information (per serving): Calories: 130 kcal; Protein: 2 g; Carbohydrates: 22 g; Fats: 3 g; Fiber: 1 g; Cholesterol: 0 mg; Sodium: 10 mg; Potassium: 40 mg

# Vanilla Cashew Cream Pudding with Pomegranate

*Prep. time: 10 min (plus 4 hours for soaking cashews) | Setting Time: 10 min | Serves: 2*

Ingredients:
- ½ cup raw cashews
- ⅓ cup unsweetened almond milk or other plant-based milk
- 1 tbsp maple syrup (adjust to taste)
- ½ tsp vanilla bean paste or pure vanilla extract
- ⅛ tsp ground cinnamon
- ¼ cup pomegranate arils (for garnish)
- 1 tsp pomegranate juice (for garnish)

Directions:
1. Soak raw cashews in water for at least 4 hours or overnight. Drain and rinse well before using.
2. In a high-speed blender, combine cashews, almond milk, maple syrup, vanilla bean paste and cinnamon. Blend until smooth and creamy, scraping down the sides as needed.
3. Taste mixture and add more maple syrup, if desired. If the cream is too thick, add a teaspoon of almond milk at a time to reach desired pudding-like consistency.
4. Transfer cashew cream pudding into two small serving bowls or ramekins. Chill in the refrigerator for at least 30 minutes to set.
5. Before serving, top each pudding with a sprinkle of pomegranate arils and a drizzle of pomegranate juice.

Nutritional Information (per serving): Calories: 220 kcal; Protein: 5 g; Carbohydrates: 20 g; Fats: 13 g; Fiber: 2 g; Cholesterol: 0 mg; Sodium: 10 mg; Potassium: 190 mg

# Vegan Orange and Almond Cake

*Prep. time: 15 min | Cook Time: 30 min | Serves: 2*

Ingredients:
- ½ cup almond flour
- ¼ cup whole wheat pastry flour or all-purpose flour
- ¼ tsp baking soda
- ¼ tsp baking powder
- ⅛ tsp salt
- ¼ cup freshly squeezed orange juice
- 1 tbsp orange zest
- 2 tbsp maple syrup or agave syrup
- 1 tbsp unsweetened almond milk or other plant-based milk
- ½ tsp vanilla extract
- 1 tbsp slivered almonds (for garnish)

Directions:
1. Preheat your oven to 175°C (350°F). Grease a 6-inch round cake pan or line it with parchment paper.
2. In a medium bowl, whisk together almond flour, whole wheat flour, baking soda, baking powder and salt.
3. In another bowl, mix orange juice, orange zest, maple syrup, almond milk and vanilla extract until combined.
4. Gradually pour the wet ingredients into the dry ingredients. Stir gently until just combined; do not overmix.
5. Pour batter into the prepared cake pan. Smooth top with a spatula.
6. Bake in the preheated oven for 25-30 minutes or until a toothpick inserted into the center comes out clean.
7. Allow cake to cool in the pan for 5 minutes, then transfer to a wire rack to cool completely. Garnish with slivered almonds or a dusting of orange zest before serving.

Nutritional Information (per serving): Calories: 180 kcal; Protein: 4 g; Carbohydrates: 20 g; Fats: 8 g; Fiber: 3 g; Cholesterol: 0 mg; Sodium: 90 mg; Potassium: 140 mg

# Lemon and Blueberry Polenta Cake

*Prep. time: 15 min | Cook Time: 30 min | Serves: 2*

Ingredients:
- ¼ cup polenta (coarse cornmeal)
- 2 tbsp almond flour
- ¼ tsp baking powder
- 2 tbsp maple syrup
- ¼ cup unsweetened almond milk
- 1 tsp lemon zest
- 1 tbsp fresh lemon juice
- ¼ cup fresh or frozen blueberries
- A sprinkle of powdered sugar substitute
- Pinch of salt

Directions:
1. Preheat oven to 175°C (350°F). Lightly grease two small ramekins or a mini cake pan.
2. In a mixing bowl, whisk together polenta, almond flour, baking powder and salt.
3. In another bowl, mix maple syrup, almond milk, lemon zest and lemon juice until well combined.
4. Slowly pour the wet ingredients into the dry ingredients, stirring until just combined. Gently fold in blueberries, being careful not to overmix.
5. Divide batter evenly between ramekins or pour into the mini cake pan. Bake for 25-30 minutes or until a toothpick inserted in the center comes out clean.
6. Allow cakes to cool for 5 minutes before removing from the ramekins or pan. Serve warm or at room temperature, garnished with powdered sugar substitute, fresh blueberries or a lemon wedge, if desired.

Nutritional Information (per serving): Calories: 160 kcal; Protein: 3 g; Carbohydrates: 25 g; Fats: 4 g; Fiber: 2 g; Cholesterol: 0 mg; Sodium: 50 mg; Potassium: 75 mg

# Cinnamon-Spiced Roasted Almond Butter Bark

*Prep. time: 10 min | Setting Time: 30 min (to chill) | Serves: 2*

Ingredients:
- ¼ cup unsweetened almond butter
- 1 tbsp coconut oil, melted
- 1 tbsp maple syrup (adjust to taste)
- ½ tsp ground cinnamon
- ¼ tsp vanilla extract
- 2 tbsp roasted almonds, roughly chopped
- 1 tbsp shredded coconut
- Pinch of sea salt

Directions:
1. In a small bowl, combine almond butter, melted coconut oil, maple syrup, ground cinnamon and vanilla extract. Stir until smooth and well combined.
2. Line a small baking tray with parchment paper. Pour almond butter mixture onto it and spread to about ¼-inch thickness. Sprinkle chopped roasted almonds, shredded coconut and a pinch of sea salt.
3. Place tray in the freezer for 30 minutes or until the bark is firm.
4. Once set, remove the bark from the freezer and peel off the parchment paper. Break the bark into bite-sized pieces. Enjoy immediately or store in an airtight container in the refrigerator for up to a week.

Nutritional Information (per serving): Calories: 180 kcal; Protein: 4 g; Carbohydrates: 8 g; Fats: 15 g; Fiber: 3 g; Cholesterol: 0 mg; Sodium: 15 mg; Potassium: 150 mg

# Vegan Espresso Almond Truffles Recipe

*Prep. time: 15 min | Chilling Time: 20 min | Serves: 2*

Ingredients:
- ½ cup almonds, finely ground
- 2 tbsp almond butter
- 2 tbsp unsweetened cacao powder
- 1 tbsp brewed espresso, cooled
- 1 tbsp maple syrup or liquid sweetener of choice
- ¼ tsp vanilla extract
- 1-2 tbsp almond flour (for rolling)

Directions:
1. In a medium bowl, combine ground almonds, almond butter, cocoa powder, brewed espresso, maple syrup and vanilla extract Mix well until a sticky dough forms.
2. Use your hands or a small cookie scoop to form mixture into bite-sized balls, about 1 inch in diameter.
3. Roll each truffle in almond flour to coat evenly.
4. Place truffles on a parchment-lined plate or tray and refrigerate for 20 minutes to firm up.
5. Arrange truffles on a serving dish. Optionally, dust lightly with extra cocoa powder and serve.

Nutritional Information (per serving): Calories: 200 kcal; Protein: 6 g; Carbohydrates: 10 g; Fats: 16 g; Fiber: 4 g; Cholesterol: 0 mg; Sodium: 5 mg; Potassium: 160 mg

# Almond Milk Panna Cotta with Raspberry Coulis

*Prep. time: 10 min | Cook Time: 5 min | Setting Time: 2-3 hours | Serves: 2*

Ingredients:
- 1 cup unsweetened almond milk
- 2 tbsp maple syrup
- ½ tsp vanilla extract
- ½ tsp agar-agar powder or 1 tsp powdered gelatine
- ½ cup fresh or frozen raspberries
- 1 tbsp maple syrup
- 1 tsp fresh lemon juice
- Fresh raspberries (for garnish)
- Fresh mint leaves (for garnish)

Directions:
1. In a small saucepan, combine almond milk, maple syrup and vanilla extract. Whisk well.
2. Sprinkle agar-agar powder over the mixture and whisk until dissolved. Let it sit for 1 minute.
3. Place saucepan over medium heat and bring to a gentle simmer, whisking constantly. Cook for 2-3 minutes until agar-agar is fully activated and mixture thickens slightly.
4. Pour mixture evenly into two small ramekins or serving glasses. Allow to cool to room temperature, then refrigerate for 2-3 hours until fully set.
5. In a small saucepan, combine raspberries, maple syrup and lemon juice. Cook over medium heat for 5 minutes, stirring and mashing raspberries with a spoon.
6. Strain raspberry coulis through a fine mesh sieve to remove seeds, if desired. Allow to cool.
7. Once panna cotta is set, spoon raspberry coulis over the top, garnish with fresh raspberries and mint leaves and serve.

Nutritional Information (per serving): Calories: 120 kcal; Protein: 1 g; Carbohydrates: 18 g; Fats: 3 g; Fiber: 2 g; Cholesterol: 0 mg; Sodium: 20 mg; Potassium: 140 mg

# Heart-Smart Smoothies & Sips

# Raspberry and Mint Lemonade Smoothie

*Prep. time: 5 min | Serves: 2*

Ingredients:
- 1 cup raspberries, fresh or frozen
- 1 tbsp freshly squeezed lemon juice
- ½ cup unsweetened coconut water
- ½ cup unsweetened plain coconut yogurt
- 1 tbsp fresh mint leaves
- ¼ tsp freshly grated ginger
- 1 tsp honey or maple syrup (optional)
- ½ cup ice cubes (optional)

Directions:
1. Rinse raspberries and mint leaves thoroughly. Juice lemon and grate ginger.
2. Add raspberries, lemon juice, coconut water, coconut yogurt, mint leaves and grated ginger to a blender.
3. Blend on high speed until all ingredients are fully combined and smoothie has a creamy, vibrant pink texture.
4. Taste smoothie and, if needed, add honey or maple syrup for extra sweetness. Add ice cubes for a thicker and colder texture and blend again.
5. Pour smoothie into two glasses, garnish with a sprig of mint and serve immediately.

*Can be served as a revitalizing breakfast drink, a pre-workout boost or a refreshing mid-afternoon snack.

Nutritional Information (per serving): Calories: 120 kcal; Protein: 2 g; Carbohydrates: 20 g; Fats: 2 g; Fiber: 5 g; Cholesterol: 0 mg; Sodium: 15 mg; Potassium: 250 mg

# Blueberry Oatmeal Breakfast Smoothie

*Prep. time: 5 min | Setting Time (Optional for Oat Soaking): 10 minutes | Serves: 2*

Ingredients:
- ½ cup fresh or frozen blueberries
- ¼ cup rolled oats
- 1 cup unsweetened almond milk or another plant-based milk
- ½ cup unsweetened plain coconut yogurt
- 1 medium banana, ripe
- ½ tsp ground cinnamon
- 1 tbsp chia seeds
- 1 tsp honey or maple syrup (optional)
- ½ cup ice cubes (optional)

Directions:
1. For a smoother texture, soak rolled oats in almond milk for 10 minutes before blending. This step is optional but enhances the creaminess.
2. Wash blueberries. Peel and slice the banana.
3. Add soaked oats or dry oats, if skipping the soaking step, almond milk, blueberries, coconut yogurt, banana, ground cinnamon and chia seeds into the blender.
4. Add ice cubes for a cooler, thicker smoothie. If desired, add honey or maple syrup for a touch of sweetness.
5. Blend on high speed until the mixture is smooth and creamy.
6. Pour smoothie into two glasses and garnish with a sprinkle of cinnamon or a few fresh blueberries for an appealing presentation.

*Serve as a quick breakfast alongside a handful of nuts or seeds for a complete, cholesterol-friendly meal.

Nutritional Information (per serving): Calories: 190 kcal; Protein: 4 g; Carbohydrates: 34 g; Fats: 3 g; Fiber: 6 g; Cholesterol: 0 mg; Sodium: 50 mg; Potassium: 300 mg

# Tropical Pineapple and Spinach Smoothie Recipe
*Prep. time: 5 min | Serves: 2*

Ingredients:
- 1 cup fresh or frozen pineapple chunks
- 1 cup fresh baby spinach leaves
- ½ banana, sliced and frozen
- ½ cup unsweetened coconut water
- ½ cup unsweetened almond milk
- 1 tsp chia seeds
- ½ tsp fresh lime zest
- ¼ tsp pure vanilla extract

Directions:
1. In a blender, add pineapple chunks, spinach, banana, coconut water, almond milk, chia seeds, lime zest and vanilla extract. If using fresh pineapple or banana, freeze them for at least 1 hour.
2. Blend on high speed until smooth and creamy, scraping down the sides as needed.
3. Taste smoothie and adjust sweetness by adding a small amount of natural sweetener like maple syrup.
4. Pour smoothie into two glasses, garnish with a sprinkle of chia seeds and serve immediately.

Nutritional Information (per serving): Calories: 95 kcal; Protein: 2 g; Carbohydrates: 20 g; Fats: 1 g; Fiber: 3 g; Cholesterol: 0 mg; Sodium: 60 mg; Potassium: 320 mg

# Berry Burst Chia Smoothie
*Prep. time: 5 min | Serves: 2*

Ingredients:
- 1 cup mixed fresh or frozen berries
- 1 tbsp chia seeds
- ½ cup unsweetened almond milk
- ½ cup plain coconut yogurt
- 1 tbsp maple syrup (optional)
- ½ tsp vanilla extract
- ½ cup ice cubes (optional)
- 1 small banana (optional)

Directions:
1. In a blender, add mixed berries, chia seeds, almond milk, coconut yogurt, vanilla extract and maple syrup.
2. Add ice cubes for a thicker consistency or banana for creaminess, depending on your preference.
3. Blend on high speed until mixture is smooth and creamy. Stop to scrape down the sides, if needed.
4. Pour into two glasses and serve fresh for the best flavour and nutritional benefits.

Nutritional Information (per serving): Calories: 120 kcal; Protein: 2 g; Carbohydrates: 22 g; Fats: 3 g; Fiber: 5 g; Cholesterol: 0 mg; Sodium: 40 mg; Potassium: 200 mg

# Green Detox Smoothie with Cucumber and Kiwi
*Prep. time: 5 min | Serves: 2*

Ingredients:
- 1 cup cucumber, peeled and chopped
- 2 kiwis, peeled and chopped
- ½ cup unsweetened coconut water
- ½ cup baby spinach leaves
- 1 small green apple, cored and chopped
- 1 tbsp chia seeds
- ¼ cup fresh mint leaves
- ½ cup ice cubes (optional)

Directions:
1. Peel and chop cucumber, kiwis and green apple. Rinse spinach and mint leaves thoroughly.
2. Add cucumber, kiwis, coconut water, spinach, green apple, chia seeds and mint leaves to a blender.
3. Add ice cubes if a colder texture is desired and blend again.
4. Blend on high speed until mixture is smooth and creamy.
5. Pour into two glasses and garnish with a sprig of mint or a slice of kiwi.

Nutritional Information (per serving): Calories: 110 kcal; Protein: 2 g; Carbohydrates: 22 g; Fats: 1 g; Fiber: 4 g; Cholesterol: 0 mg; Sodium: 15 mg; Potassium: 300 mg

# Carrot Ginger Immunity Smoothie
*Prep. time: 5 min | Serves: 2*

Ingredients:
- 1 cup fresh carrot juice, store-bought or homemade
- 1 medium orange, peeled and segmented
- 1 small banana, ripe
- ½ cup unsweetened almond milk or any plant-based milk
- ½ tsp freshly grated ginger
- ¼ tsp ground turmeric
- ½ tsp lemon juice (optional)
- 1 tbsp chia seeds (optional)
- ½ cup ice cubes (optional)
- 1 tsp honey or maple syrup (optional)

Directions:
1. If not using pre-made carrot juice, blend fresh carrots with a little water and strain the juice through a fine mesh sieve or cheesecloth. Peel and segment the orange.
2. Add carrot juice, orange segments, banana, almond milk, ginger, turmeric and lemon juice, if using, into the blender.
3. Add chia seeds and ice cubes for a thicker and cooler smoothie. If additional sweetness is desired, add honey or maple syrup.
4. Blend on high speed until all ingredients are fully combined, and smoothie has a creamy, bright orange texture.
5. Pour into two glasses and garnish with a sprinkle of chia seeds or a dash of turmeric.

Nutritional Information (per serving): Calories: 130 kcal; Protein: 2 g; Carbohydrates: 29 g; Fats: 2 g; Fiber: 5 g; Cholesterol: 0 mg; Sodium: 60 mg; Potassium: 350 mg

# Zesty Lemon Kale Smoothie
*Prep. time: 5 min | Serves: 2*

Ingredients:
- 1 cup fresh kale leaves (packed), stems removed
- 1 small green apple, cored and chopped
- ½ medium banana, ripe
- 1 tbsp freshly squeezed lemon juice
- ½ tsp lemon zest
- ½ cup unsweetened almond milk or any plant-based milk
- ½ cup water
- ½ tsp grated ginger (optional)
- 1 tbsp chia seeds (optional)
- ½ cup ice cubes (optional)

Directions:
1. Wash and destem kale leaves. Core and chop green apple. Peel and slice banana. Zest and juice lemon.
2. Add kale, green apple, banana, lemon juice, lemon zest, almond milk and water into a blender.
3. Add grated ginger, chia seeds and ice cubes for added flavour and texture.
4. Blend on high speed until mixture is smooth and creamy, with no visible chunks of kale.
5. Pour smoothie into two glasses and garnish with a slice of lemon or a sprinkle of chia seeds.

Nutritional Information (per serving): Calories: 110 kcal; Protein: 3 g; Carbohydrates: 23 g; Fats: 2 g; Fiber: 5 g; Cholesterol: 0 mg; Sodium: 50 mg; Potassium: 300 mg

# Matcha Green Tea and Banana Smoothie

*Prep. time: 5 min | Serves: 2*

Ingredients:
- ½ tsp matcha green tea powder
- 1 medium banana, ripe
- ½ cup unsweetened almond milk
- ½ cup unsweetened plain coconut yogurt
- ½ tsp ground cinnamon
- 1 tbsp chia seeds
- 1 tsp honey or maple syrup (optional)
- ½ cup ice cubes (optional)

Directions:
1. Add matcha powder, banana, almond milk, coconut yogurt, cinnamon and chia seeds to the blender.
2. Add ice cubes for a thicker, colder smoothie. If additional sweetness is needed, add honey or maple syrup.
3. Blend on high speed until mixture is creamy and evenly combined.
4. Pour into two glasses and garnish with a light dusting of cinnamon or matcha powder.

Nutritional Information (per serving): Calories: 120 kcal; Protein: 2 g; Carbohydrates: 22 g; Fats: 2 g; Fiber: 4 g; Cholesterol: 0 mg; Sodium: 40 mg; Potassium: 300 mg

# Orange Sunshine Smoothie with Turmeric

*Prep. time: 5 min | Serves: 2*

Ingredients:
- 1 cup freshly squeezed orange juice
- ½ medium banana
- ½ cup unsweetened almond milk
- ½ cup unsweetened plain coconut yogurt
- ¼ tsp ground turmeric
- ¼ tsp ground cinnamon
- ½ tsp grated ginger
- ½ cup ice cubes (optional)

Directions:
1. Add orange juice, banana, almond milk, coconut yogurt, turmeric, cinnamon, ginger and ice cubes into a blender.
2. Blend on high speed until all ingredients are fully combined, resulting in a creamy, smooth texture.
3. Pour into two glasses and garnish with a light sprinkle of turmeric or a slice of orange.

Nutritional Information (per serving): Calories: 120 kcal; Protein: 2 g; Carbohydrates: 23 g; Fats: 2 g; Fiber: 3 g; Cholesterol: 0 mg; Sodium: 35 mg; Potassium: 300 mg

# Spiced Pumpkin Pie Smoothie

*Prep. time: 5 min | Serves: 2*

Ingredients:
- ½ cup canned unsweetened pumpkin puree
- 1 medium banana
- 1 cup unsweetened almond milk
- ½ cup unsweetened plain coconut yogurt
- ½ tsp ground cinnamon
- ¼ tsp ground nutmeg
- 1 tbsp maple syrup (optional)
- ½ cup ice cubes (optional)

Directions:
1. Add pumpkin puree, banana, almond milk, coconut yogurt, cinnamon, nutmeg and maple syrup into a blender.
2. Add ice cubes for a colder, thicker consistency, if desired.
3. Blend on high speed until all ingredients are fully combined, creating a creamy and smooth texture.
4. Pour into two glasses and garnish with a light sprinkle of cinnamon or nutmeg and serve.

Nutritional Information (per serving): Calories: 140 kcal; Protein: 2 g; Carbohydrates: 26 g; Fats: 2 g; Fiber: 4 g; Cholesterol: 0 mg; Sodium: 40 mg; Potassium: 350 mg

# Golden Turmeric Almond Latte

*Prep. time: 5 min | Cook Time: 5 min | Serves: 2*

Ingredients:
- 2 cups unsweetened almond milk
- 1 tsp ground turmeric
- ½ tsp ground cinnamon
- ¼ tsp ground ginger
- ⅛ tsp ground black pepper
- 1 tsp maple syrup or honey
- ½ tsp vanilla extract
- ¼ cup hot water (to dissolve spices smoothly)

Directions:
1. In a small bowl, combine the turmeric, cinnamon, ginger and black pepper.
2. Heat ¼ cup of hot water in a saucepan over medium heat. Whisk in spice mix until fully dissolved to create a smooth paste.
3. Gradually pour in almond milk, stirring constantly to combine. Reduce heat to low and let mixture warm up, ensuring it doesn't boil.
4. Stir in maple syrup or honey and vanilla extract.
5. For a frothy texture, transfer mixture to a blender or a milk frother. Blend for 30 seconds until frothy.
6. Pour into two mugs and sprinkle a pinch of cinnamon or turmeric on top for a decorative touch.

Nutritional Information (per serving): Calories: 70 kcal; Protein: 1 g; Carbohydrates: 7 g; Fats: 3 g; Fiber: 1 g; Cholesterol: 0 mg; Sodium: 80 mg; Potassium: 150 mg

# Iced Hibiscus and Pomegranate Tea

*Prep. time: 5 min | Cook Time: 10 min | Cooling Time: 15 min | Serves: 2*

Ingredients:
- 2 tbsp dried hibiscus flowers
- 1 cup boiling water
- ½ cup 100% unsweetened pomegranate juice
- 1 tsp fresh lime juice
- 1 tbsp honey or maple syrup (optional)
- 4-6 fresh mint leaves
- 1 cup cold water
- 1 cup ice cubes

Directions:
1. Place dried hibiscus flowers in a heatproof bowl or teapot. Pour boiling water over them and let steep for 10 minutes.
2. Strain tea to remove hibiscus flowers and let it cool to room temperature, about 15 minutes.
3. In a large pitcher, mix cooled hibiscus tea with pomegranate juice, lime juice and honey or maple syrup. Stir until honey or syrup is fully dissolved.
4. Lightly crush mint leaves with your fingers to release their flavour and add them to the pitcher. Stir in cold water.
5. Fill two glasses with ice cubes and pour hibiscus-pomegranate tea over the ice.
6. Garnish each glass with a mint sprig or a slice of lime for an elegant touch.
   *This tea can also be served warm without adding ice.

Nutritional Information (per serving): Calories: 40 kcal; Protein: 0 g; Carbohydrates: 10 g; Fats: 0 g; Fiber: 0 g; Cholesterol: 0 mg; Sodium: 5 mg; Potassium: 100 mg

# Minty Cucumber Cooler

*Prep. time: 10 min | Serves: 2*

Ingredients:
- 1 large cucumber, peeled and chopped
- ¼ cup fresh mint leaves
- 1 tsp freshly grated ginger
- 1 tbsp freshly squeezed lime juice
- 1 tsp honey or maple syrup (optional)
- 1 cup cold water
- 1 cup ice cubes
- Mint sprigs (for garnish)

Directions:
1. Peel and chop cucumber into small pieces for easy blending. Rinse mint leaves and grate ginger.
2. Add cucumber, mint leaves, grated ginger, lime juice, honey or maple syrup and cold water into a blender.
3. Blend until smooth. For a smoother drink, strain mixture through a fine mesh sieve to remove any pulp.
4. Fill two glasses with ice cubes, pour cucumber cooler, garnish with a sprig of mint and serve.

Nutritional Information (per serving): Calories: 30 kcal; Protein: 1 g; Carbohydrates: 7 g; Fats: 0 g; Fiber: 1 g; Cholesterol: 0 mg; Sodium: 5 mg; Potassium: 150 mg

# Cranberry Ginger Fizz

*Prep. time: 5 min | Cook Time: 5 min | Serves: 2*

Ingredients:
- ½ cup 100% unsweetened cranberry juice
- ½ tsp freshly grated ginger
- 1 cup sparkling water
- 1 tsp honey or maple syrup
- 1 tsp fresh lime juice
- 2 small sprigs of fresh rosemary (for garnish)
- Ice cubes (optional)

Directions:
1. In a small saucepan, combine grated ginger with ¼ cup water. Bring to a gentle simmer for 2–3 minutes, then strain to remove ginger pulp. Let it cool.
2. In a pitcher or mixing bowl, combine cranberry juice, lime juice and cooled ginger infusio. Add honey or maple syrup, if a sweeter flavour is desired.
3. Just before serving, gently stir in sparkling water to retain the fizz.
4. Fill two glasses with ice cubes, pour cranberry ginger mixture and garnish with a rosemary sprig.

Nutritional Information (per serving): Calories: 40 kcal; Protein: 0 g; Carbohydrates: 10 g; Fats: 0 g; Fiber: 0 g; Cholesterol: 0 mg; Sodium: 5 mg; Potassium: 50 mg

# Blueberry Lemon Infused Water

*Prep. time: 5 min | Setting Time: 1–2 hours (for infusion) | Serves: 2*

Ingredients:
- ½ cup fresh blueberries
- ½ lemon, thinly sliced
- 2 sprigs fresh thyme
- 3 cups cold water
- Ice cubes (optional)

Directions:
1. Rinse blueberries, lemon and thyme thoroughly. Thinly slice lemon, gently crush thyme sprigs and lightly mash blueberries.
2. In a large pitcher, add blueberries, lemon slices and thyme sprigs. Pour in cold water.
3. Stir gently to combine. Cover pitcher and refrigerate for 1–2 hours to allow flavours to meld.
4. Fill two glasses with ice cubes and pour the infused water into the glasses.
5. Garnish each glass with a small sprig of thyme or a few extra blueberries for presentation.

Nutritional Information (per serving): Calories: 5 kcal; Protein: 0 g; Carbohydrates: 1 g; Fats: 0 g; Fiber: 0 g; Cholesterol: 0 mg; Sodium: 0 mg; Potassium: 10 mg

# Chia-Infused Limeade

*Prep. Time: 5 min | Setting Time: 10 min | Serves: 2*

Ingredients:
- 2 tbsp chia seeds
- 1 cup water (for soaking chia seeds)
- ¼ cup freshly squeezed lime juice (approx. 2–3 limes)
- 1½ cups cold water
- 1–2 tsp honey or maple syrup (optional)
- 4–6 fresh mint leaves
- 1 cup ice cubes (optional)
- Lime slices and mint sprigs (for garnish)

Directions:
1. In a small bowl or jar, combine chia seeds with 1 cup of water. Stir well to prevent clumping and let it sit for 10 minutes, stirring occasionally, until mixture becomes a gel-like consistency.
2. In a pitcher, combine freshly squeezed lime juice, 1½ cups of cold water and honey or maple syrup, if using. Stir until sweetener is fully dissolved.
3. Stir prepared chia gel into the limeade, ensuring even distribution.
4. Lightly crush mint leaves with your fingers to release their aroma, then stir them into the limeade.
5. Fill two glasses with ice cubes and pour chia-infused limeade over the ice.
6. Garnish each glass with a slice of lime and a sprig of mint for a refreshing presentation.

Nutritional Information (per serving): Calories: 50 kcal; Protein: 1 g; Carbohydrates: 11 g; Fats: 1 g; Fiber: 3 g; Cholesterol: 0 mg; Sodium: 5 mg; Potassium: 100 mg

# Zesty Grapefruit and Ginger Spritz

*Prep. time: 5 min | Serves: 2*

Ingredients:
- 1 cup freshly squeezed grapefruit juice (approx. 2 grapefruits)
- ½ cup sparkling water
- ½ tsp freshly grated ginger
- 1 tsp honey or maple syrup
- 1 sprig fresh rosemary
- 1 tbsp freshly squeezed lime juice
- 2 tbsp 100% unsweetened cranberry juice
- Ice cubes (optional)
- Grapefruit wedges and rosemary sprigs (for garnish)

Directions:
1. Peel and grate a small piece of fresh ginger using a fine grater.
2. In a pitcher, combine freshly grated ginger and honey or maple syrup. Stir to dissolve the sweetener.
3. Add freshly squeezed lime juice to the pitcher. Stir well to combine.
4. Cut grapefruits in half and juice them. Strain juice through a fine mesh sieve to remove any pulp or seeds.
5. Add freshly squeezed grapefruit juice and cranberry juice to the pitcher.
6. Take fresh sprig of rosemary and lightly crush it with your fingers to release its natural oils. Add it to the pitcher with juice mixture and let it sit for 2–3 minutes for a subtle herbal infusion.
7. Just before serving, gently stir in sparkling water to retain its fizz.
8. Fill two glasses with ice cubes, pour spritz and garnish with a rosemary sprig and a wedge of grapefruit.

Nutritional Information (per serving): Calories: 40 kcal; Protein: 0 g; Carbohydrates: 10 g; Fats: 0 g; Fiber: 0 g; Cholesterol: 0 mg; Sodium: 5 mg; Potassium: 100 mg

# Spiced Apple Cider Mocktail

*Prep. time: 10 min | Serves: 2*

Ingredients:
- 2 cups unsweetened apple cider
- 1 cinnamon stick
- 2 whole cloves
- ¼ tsp ground nutmeg
- ¼ tsp ground ginger
- ½ tsp freshly grated orange zest
- 1 tsp honey or maple syrup
- Fresh apple slices or cinnamon stick (for garnish)

Directions:
1. In a saucepan, combine apple cider, cinnamon stick, cloves, nutmeg, ginger and orange zest. Simmer over medium heat for 8–10 minutes, stirring occasionally.
2. Stir in honey or maple syrup, if desired, and adjust sweetness to taste.
3. Strain cider into two heatproof mugs and garnish with apple slices or cinnamon sticks.

Nutritional Information (per serving): Calories: 90 kcal; Protein: 0 g; Carbohydrates: 22 g; Fats: 0 g; Fiber: 1 g; Cholesterol: 0 mg; Sodium: 10 mg; Potassium: 180 mg

# Beet and Berry Antioxidant Juice

*Prep. time: 5 min | Serves: 2*

Ingredients:
- 1 medium beet, peeled and chopped
- 1 cup mixed berries (blueberries, raspberries, strawberries)
- ½ cup water
- 1 tbsp freshly squeezed lime juice
- 1 tsp honey or maple syrup (optional)
- Ice cubes (optional)

Directions:
1. Peel and chop beet into small pieces for easy blending. Wash berries thoroughly.
2. Add beet, mixed berries, water and lime juice to a blender. Blend on high speed until smooth.
3. If a smoother juice is desired, strain mixture through a fine mesh sieve or nut milk bag to remove pulp.
4. Stir in honey or maple syrup to adjust sweetness to your taste.
5. Pour juice into two glasses over ice cubes, if desired, and serve immediately.

Nutritional Information (per serving): Calories: 80 kcal; Protein: 1 g; Carbohydrates: 18 g; Fats: 0 g; Fiber: 3 g; Cholesterol: 0 mg; Sodium: 30 mg; Potassium: 280 mg

# Pear Cardamom Shake

*Prep. time: 5 min | Serves: 2*

Ingredients:
- 1 large ripe pear, cored and chopped
- ½ cup unsweetened almond milk
- ¼ cup unsweetened plain coconut yogurt
- ¼ tsp ground cardamom
- ½ tsp pure vanilla extract
- ½ tsp honey or maple syrup (optional)
- ½ cup ice cubes (optional)

Directions:
1. Wash, core and chop pear into small pieces for easy blending.
2. In a blender, combine chopped pear, almond milk, coconut yogurt, cardamom, vanilla extract and honey or maple syrup.
3. Add ice cubes if a chilled, thicker shake is desired. Blend on high speed until smooth and creamy.
4. Pour shake into two glasses and garnish with a light sprinkle of cardamom.

Nutritional Information (per serving): Calories: 90 kcal; Protein: 1 g; Carbohydrates: 18 g; Fats: 2 g; Fiber: 3 g; Cholesterol: 0 mg; Sodium: 30 mg; Potassium: 180 mg

# 30-Day Low Cholesterol Meal Plan

🍽 Breakfast  🥗 Lunch  🍲 Dinner  🍪 Dessert

### Day 1
- 🍽 Banana and Walnut Whole-Grain Pancakes
- 🥗 Lentil and Spinach Soup with a Hint of Lemon
- 🍲 Baked Cod with Lemon and Herbs, served with Coconut-Lime Cauliflower Rice
- 🍪 Avocado Chocolate Mousse

### Day 2
- 🍽 Quinoa Breakfast Bowl with Nuts and Pomegranate
- 🥗 Broccoli and Cranberry Salad with Almonds
- 🍲 Sweet Potato and Lentil Curry
- 🍪 Vegan Blueberry Almond Tart

### Day 3
- 🍽 Avocado and Spinach Egg White Omelette
- 🥗 Warm Roasted Vegetable Salad with Balsamic Glaze
- 🍲 Grilled Tofu Skewers with Peanut Sauce, served with Broccoli Slaw with Sesame Dressing
- 🍪 Sugar-Free Lemon Coconut Bars

### Day 4
- 🍽 Oatmeal with Almond Milk, Cinnamon, and Pears
- 🥗 Zucchini Noodle Salad with Pesto
- 🍲 Roasted Eggplant and Chickpea Salad Bowl
- 🍪 Mango and Passionfruit Sorbet

### Day 5
- 🍽 Spinach and Mushroom Tofu Scramble
- 🥗 Tomato and Barley Soup with Thyme
- 🍲 Moroccan Chickpea and Vegetable Tagine
- 🍪 Baked Cinnamon Pears with Walnuts

### Day 6
- 🍽 Carrot Cake Overnight Oats
- 🥗 Herb-Roasted Potato Salad
- 🍲 Roasted Cauliflower Steaks with Chimichurri, served with Baked Sweet Potato Wedges with Smoked Paprika
- 🍪 Roasted Cherry and Almond Crisp

### Day 7
- 🍽 Sweet Potato and Kale Breakfast Hash
- 🥗 Edamame and Brown Rice Salad
- 🍲 Vegan Shepherd's Pie with Lentils and Sweet Potato
- 🍪 Vegan Apple Crumble with Oats

### Day 8
- 🍽 Zucchini and Red Pepper Breakfast Muffins
- 🥗 Corn and Sweet Potato Chowder
- 🍲 Baked Eggplant Parmesan, served with Smashed Baby Potatoes with Garlic and Chives
- 🍪 Apricot and Quinoa Cookies

### Day 9
- 🍽 Green Smoothie Bowl with Granola and Kiwi
- 🥗 Split Pea Soup with Fresh Herbs
- 🍲 Cauliflower Fried Rice with Tofu
- 🍪 Sweet Potato Brownies with Cocoa

### Day 10
- 🍽 Berry and Almond Butter Breakfast Wrap
- 🥗 Spinach and Strawberry Salad with Balsamic Glaze, served with Spicy Roasted Chickpeas
- 🍲 Hearty Vegetable and Lentil Stew
- 🍪 Almond and Date Energy Bars

### Day 11
- 🍽 Pumpkin and Oat Breakfast Porridge
- 🥗 Summer Gazpacho with Fresh Herbs
- 🍲 Teriyaki Tofu Stir-Fry with Brown Rice
- 🍪 Cinnamon-Spiced Roasted Almond Butter Bark

### Day 12
- 🍽 Lentil and Veggie Breakfast Scramble
- 🥗 Roasted Garlic and Mushroom Soup
- 🍲 Roasted Vegetable Buddha Bowl with Tahini Dressing
- 🍪 Sesame and Coconut Mochi Bites

### Day 13
- 🍽 Sweet Corn and Zucchini Breakfast Fritters
- 🥗 Thai-Inspired Cabbage Slaw with Peanut Dressing, served with Crispy Baked Tofu Nuggets
- 🍲 Butternut Squash and Kale Risotto
- 🍪 Vegan Espresso Almond Truffles

### Day 14
- 🍽 Veggie-Packed Savoury Oatmeal
- 🥗 Broccoli and Pea Soup with Fresh Mint
- 🍲 Quinoa-Stuffed Bell Peppers with Chickpeas served with Cauliflower Mash with Fresh Thyme
- 🍪 Vegan Orange and Almond Cake

### Day 15
- 🍽 Buckwheat Pancakes with Warm Berry Compote
- 🥗 Cabbage and White Bean Soup
- 🍲 Baked Salmon with Garlic, Dill and Asparagus, served with Roasted Carrot and Parsnip Medley
- 🍪 Almond Milk Panna Cotta with Raspberry Coulis

# 30-Day Low Cholesterol Meal Plan

### Day 16
- 🍲 Walnut and Date Breakfast Bars
- 🥗 Mixed Greens with Orange and Pumpkin Seeds, served with Roasted Bell Pepper Hummus with Pita Wedges
- 🍛 Mushroom and Barley Stuffed Cabbage Rolls
- 🍪 Chocolate-Covered Dates with Almond Butter Filling

### Day 17
- 🍲 Baked Oatmeal Cups with Blueberries and Walnuts
- 🥗 Roasted Beet and Avocado Salad, served with Baked Polenta Fries with Marinara Dip
- 🍛 Sweet Potato and Black Bean Enchiladas
- 🍪 Vegan Chocolate Banana Bread

### Day 18
- 🍲 Quinoa Bowl with Sautéed Kale and Mushrooms
- 🥗 Cauliflower and Leek Soup with Garlic Croutons
- 🍛 Moroccan Chickpea and Vegetable Tagine
- 🍪 Vanilla Cashew Cream Pudding with Pomegranate

### Day 19
- 🍲 Carrot Cake Overnight Oats
- 🥗 Zesty Bean and Corn Salad
- 🍛 Roasted Portobello Mushrooms with Brown Rice
- 🍪 Roasted Cherry and Almond Crisp

### Day 20
- 🍲 Sweet Potato Bowl with Almonds and Cinnamon
- 🥗 Quinoa and Kale Detox Soup
- 🍛 Broccoli and Cashew Stir-Fry with Brown Rice
- 🍪 Mango and Passionfruit Sorbet

### Day 21
- 🍲 Veggie-Packed Breakfast Burrito
- 🥗 Herb-Infused Brown Rice Pilaf, served with Balsamic Glazed Roasted Pearl Onions
- 🍛 Baked Cod with Lemon and Herbs, served with Cauliflower Mash with Fresh Thyme
- 🍪 Sugar-Free Lemon Coconut Bars

### Day 22
- 🍲 Green Smoothie Bowl with Granola and Kiwi
- 🥗 Lentil and Spinach Soup with a Hint of Lemon
- 🍛 Roasted Cauliflower Steaks with Chimichurri, served with Coconut-Lime Cauliflower Rice
- 🍪 Vegan Apple Crumble with Oats

### Day 23
- 🍲 Avocado and Spinach Egg White Omelette
- 🥗 Broccoli and Cranberry Salad with Almonds, served with Garlic and Herb Roasted Mushrooms
- 🍛 Teriyaki Tofu Stir-Fry with Brown Rice
- 🍪 Chocolate-Covered Dates with Almond Butter Filling

### Day 24
- 🍲 Pumpkin and Oat Breakfast Porridge
- 🥗 Tomato and Barley Soup with Thyme
- 🍛 Grilled Tofu Skewers with Peanut Sauce, served with Sesame Green Beans with Soy Glaze
- 🍪 Roasted Cherry and Almond Crisp

### Day 25
- 🍲 Sweet Potato and Kale Breakfast Hash
- 🥗 Zucchini Noodle Salad with Pesto
- 🍛 Sweet Potato and Black Bean Enchiladas
- 🍪 Vanilla Cashew Cream Pudding with Pomegranate

### Day 26
- 🍲 Carrot Cake Overnight Oats
- 🥗 Herb-Roasted Potato Salad (No Mayo)
- 🍛 Baked Eggplant Parmesan, served with Baked Sweet Potato Wedges with Smoked Paprika
- 🍪 Mango and Passionfruit Sorbet

### Day 27
- 🍲 Quinoa Breakfast Bowl with Nuts and Pomegranate
- 🥗 Roasted Garlic and Mushroom Soup
- 🍛 Roasted Vegetable Buddha Bowl with Tahini Dressing
- 🍪 Sugar-Free Lemon Coconut Bars

### Day 28
- 🍲 Lentil and Veggie Breakfast Scramble
- 🥗 Spinach and Strawberry Salad with Balsamic Glaze, served with Baked Zucchini Sticks with Marinara Sauce
- 🍛 Baked Salmon with Garlic, Dill and Asparagus, served with Roasted Carrot and Parsnip Medley
- 🍪 Vegan Blueberry Almond Tart

### Day 29
- 🍲 Berry and Almond Butter Breakfast Wrap
- 🥗 Broccoli and Pea Soup with Fresh Mint
- 🍛 Moroccan Chickpea and Vegetable Tagine
- 🍪 Vegan Espresso Almond Truffles

### Day 30
- 🍲 Walnut and Date Breakfast Bars
- 🥗 Warm Roasted Vegetable Salad with Balsamic Glaze
- 🍛 Mushroom and Barley Stuffed Cabbage Rolls
- 🍪 Sweet Potato Brownies with Cocoa

**Your Thoughts Matter**

As you reach the end of this cookbook, I hope you've found inspiration in these heart-healthy recipes and discovered new ways to enjoy flavourful, nourishing meals. Cooking is more than just preparing food - it's about creating habits that support your well-being, bringing loved ones together and making choices that contribute to a healthier life.

If this book has helped you in any way - whether by introducing new favourite meals, simplifying meal planning or making a low-cholesterol lifestyle feel more accessible - I'd love to hear about your experience. Your insights and feedback are incredibly valuable, not just for me, but for others who may be looking for the same guidance on their own journey.

If you have a moment, sharing your thoughts would mean a lot. Your experiences can help others find inspiration and confidence in their own kitchens. Let's continue spreading the joy of healthy, delicious eating together!

# Cooking Measurements & Conversions

## LIQUID MEASUREMENTS

| GALLONS | QUARTS | PINTS | CUPS | FLUIDS OZ | FLUIDS ML |
|---|---|---|---|---|---|
| 1 gal | 4 qt | 8 pt | 16 cup | 128 fl oz | 3,785 ml |
| 1/2 gal | 2 qt | 4 pt | 8 cup | 64 fl oz | 1,893 ml |
| 1/4 gal | 1 qt | 2 pt | 4 cup | 32 fl oz | 946 ml |
| 1/8 gal | 1/2 qt | 1 pt | 2 cup | 16 fl oz | 473 ml |
| 1/16 gal | 1/4 qt | 1/2 pt | 1 cup | 8 fl oz | 237 ml |

## DRY MEASUREMENTS

| CUPS | TABLESPOONS | TEASPOONS | GRAMS |
|---|---|---|---|
| 1 cup | 16 tbsp | 48 tsp | 229 g |
| 1/2 cup | 8 tbsp | 24 tsp | 114 g |
| 1/3 cup | 5 tbsp | 16 tsp | 76 g |
| 1/4 cup | 4 tbsp | 12 tsp | 57 g |
| 1/8 cup | 2 tbsp | 6 tsp | 29 g |
| 1/16 cup | 1 tbsp | 3 tsp | 14 g |

## OVEN TEMPERATURES

| °C | 120 | 135 | 150 | 165 | 180 | 190 | 200 | 220 | 230 | 245 |
|---|---|---|---|---|---|---|---|---|---|---|
| °F | 250 | 275 | 300 | 325 | 350 | 375 | 400 | 425 | 450 | 475 |

# INDEX

**A**

### almond butter
Walnut and Date Breakfast Bars, 18
Berry and Almond Butter Breakfast Wrap, 19
Chocolate-Covered Dates with Almond Butter Filling, 59
Cinnamon-Spiced Roasted Almond Butter Bark, 65
Vegan Espresso Almond Truffles Recipe, 66
Sweet Potato Brownies with Cacao, 59

### almond flour
Vegan Apple Crumble with Oats, 58
Sweet Potato Brownies with Cacao, 59
Sugar-Free Lemon Coconut Bars, 60
Vegan Blueberry Almond Tart, 61
Apricot and Quinoa Cookies, 62
Roasted Cherry and Almond Crisp, 62
Vegan Orange and Almond Cake, 64
Lemon and Blueberry Polenta Cake, 65

### almond milk
Banana and Walnut Whole-Grain Pancakes, 13
Quinoa Breakfast Bowl with Nuts and Pomegranate, 14
Oatmeal with Almond Milk, Cinnamon and Pears, 15
Zucchini and Red Pepper Breakfast Muffins, 15
Green Smoothie Bowl with Granola and Kiwi, 16
Carrot Cake Overnight Oats, 17
Sweet Potato Bowl with Almonds and Cinnamon, 18
Buckwheat Pancakes with Warm Berry Compote, 20
Pumpkin and Oat Breakfast Porridge, 21
Baked Oatmeal Cups with Blueberries and Walnuts, 22
Corn and Sweet Potato Chowder, 24
Roasted Garlic and Mushroom Soup, 31
Baked Eggplant Parmesan (Dairy-Free), 36
Vegan Shepherd's Pie with Lentils and Sweet Potato, 37
Lemon and Blueberry Polenta Cake, 65
Almond Milk Panna Cotta with Raspberry Coulis, 66
Blueberry Oatmeal Breakfast Smoothie, 68
Tropical Pineapple and Spinach Smoothie Recipe, 69
Berry Burst Chia Smoothie, 69
Carrot Ginger Immunity Smoothie, 70
Matcha Green Tea and Banana Smoothie, 71
Orange Sunshine Smoothie with Turmeric, 71
Spiced Pumpkin Pie Smoothie, 71
Golden Turmeric Almond Latte, 72
Pear Cardamom Shake, 75
Cauliflower and Leek Soup with Garlic Croutons, 32
Cauliflower Mash with Fresh Thyme, 53
Vanilla Cashew Cream Pudding with Pomegranate, 64
Zesty Lemon Kale Smoothie, 70

### almonds
Almond and Date Energy Bars, 61
Vegan Espresso Almond Truffles Recipe, 66
Cinnamon-Spiced Roasted Almond Butter Bark, 65

### apple
Green Detox Smoothie with Cucumber and Kiwi, 69
Zesty Lemon Kale Smoothie, 70
Vegan Apple Crumble with Oats, 58

### apple cider
Spiced Apple Cider Mocktail, 75

### apricots
Apricot and Quinoa Cookies, 62

### asparagus
Baked Salmon with Garlic, Dill and Asparagus, 41

### avocado
Avocado and Spinach Egg White Omelette, 13
Roasted Beet and Avocado Salad, 28
Zesty Bean and Corn Salad, 32
Avocado and Lime Guacamole with Veggie Sticks, 49
Avocado Chocolate Mousse, 58
baby potatoes
Herb-Roasted Potato Salad, 29
Smashed Baby Potatoes with Garlic and Chives, 52

**B**

### banana
Banana and Walnut Whole-Grain Pancakes, 13
Green Smoothie Bowl with Granola and Kiwi, 16
Vegan Chocolate Banana Bread, 63
Blueberry Oatmeal Breakfast Smoothie, 68
Tropical Pineapple and Spinach Smoothie Recipe, 69
Berry Burst Chia Smoothie, 69
Carrot Ginger Immunity Smoothie, 70
Zesty Lemon Kale Smoothie, 70
Matcha Green Tea and Banana Smoothie, 71
Orange Sunshine Smoothie with Turmeric, 71
Spiced Pumpkin Pie Smoothie, 71

### beet
Beet and Berry Antioxidant Juice, 75
Roasted Beet and Avocado Salad, 28

### bell pepper
Sweet Potato and Kale Breakfast Hash, 14
Thai-Inspired Cabbage Slaw with Peanut Dressing, 25
Edamame and Brown Rice Salad, 27
Summer Gazpacho with Fresh Herbs, 29
Warm Roasted Vegetable Salad with Balsamic Glaze, 31
Zesty Bean and Corn Salad, 32
Teriyaki Tofu Stir-Fry with Brown Rice, 37
Stuffed Portobello Mushrooms with Brown Rice, 38
Grilled Tofu Skewers with Peanut Sauce, 39
Roasted Vegetable Buddha Bowl with Tahini Dressing, 39
Cauliflower Fried Rice with Tofu, 40
Broccoli and Cashew Stir-Fry with Brown Rice, 44
Avocado and Lime Guacamole with Veggie Sticks, 49
Sweet Corn Salad with Lime and Cilantro, 53
Roasted Bell Pepper Hummus with Pita Wedges, 55
Veggie-Packed Breakfast Burrito, 17
Lentil and Veggie Breakfast Scramble, 19
Veggie-Packed Savoury Oatmeal, 20
Quinoa-Stuffed Bell Peppers with Chickpeas, 35
Zucchini and Red Pepper Breakfast Muffins, 15

### black beans
Veggie-Packed Breakfast Burrito, 17
Zesty Bean and Corn Salad, 32
Sweet Potato and Black Bean Enchiladas, 42

### blueberries
Baked Oatmeal Cups with Blueberries and Walnuts, 22
Vegan Blueberry Almond Tart, 61
Lemon and Blueberry Polenta Cake, 65

Blueberry Oatmeal Breakfast Smoothie, 68
Blueberry Lemon Infused Water, 73
### breadcrumbs
Baked Eggplant Parmesan (Dairy-Free), 36
Crispy Baked Tofu Nuggets, 49
Baked Zucchini Sticks with Marinara Sauce, 47
### brewed espresso
Vegan Espresso Almond Truffles Recipe, 66
### broccoli
Broccoli and Cranberry Salad with Almonds, 24
Broccoli and Pea Soup with Fresh Mint, 27
Warm Roasted Vegetable Salad with Balsamic Glaze, 31
Teriyaki Tofu Stir-Fry with Brown Rice, 37
Roasted Vegetable Buddha Bowl with Tahini Dressing, 39
Cauliflower Fried Rice with Tofu, 40
Broccoli and Cashew Stir-Fry with Brown Rice, 44
### brown rice
Edamame and Brown Rice Salad, 27
Teriyaki Tofu Stir-Fry with Brown Rice, 37
Stuffed Portobello Mushrooms with Brown Rice, 38
Broccoli and Cashew Stir-Fry with Brown Rice, 44
Herb-Infused Brown Rice Pilaf, 48
### buckwheat flour
Buckwheat Pancakes with Warm Berry Compote, 20
butternut squash
Warm Roasted Vegetable Salad with Balsamic Glaze, 31
butternut squash
Butternut Squash and Kale Risotto, 43

## C

### cabbage
Thai-Inspired Cabbage Slaw with Peanut Dressing, 25
Cabbage and White Bean Soup, 26
Mushroom and Barley Stuffed Cabbage Rolls, 44
cacao powder
Sweet Potato Brownies with Cacao, 59
Avocado Chocolate Mousse, 58
Vegan Chocolate Banana Bread, 63
Vegan Espresso Almond Truffles Recipe, 66
### carrot
Carrot Cake Overnight Oats, 17
Lentil and Spinach Soup with a Hint of Lemon, 25
Edamame and Brown Rice Salad, 27
Split Pea Soup with Fresh Herbs, 33
Teriyaki Tofu Stir-Fry with Brown Rice, 37
Vegan Shepherd's Pie with Lentils and Sweet Potato, 37
Avocado and Lime Guacamole with Veggie Sticks, 49
Thai-Inspired Cabbage Slaw with Peanut Dressing, 25
Cabbage and White Bean Soup, 26
Tomato and Barley Soup with Thyme, 28
Quinoa and Kale Detox Soup, 30
Moroccan Chickpea and Vegetable Tagine, 38
Cauliflower Fried Rice with Tofu, 40
Vegan Bolognese with Whole-Grain Pasta, 41
Hearty Vegetable and Lentil Stew, 43
Roasted Carrot and Parsnip Medley, 54
### carrot juice
Carrot Ginger Immunity Smoothie, 70
### cashews
Broccoli and Cashew Stir-Fry with Brown Rice, 44
Vanilla Cashew Cream Pudding with Pomegranate, 64
### cauliflower
Cauliflower and Leek Soup with Garlic Croutons, 32
Roasted Cauliflower Steaks with Chimichurri, 36
Cauliflower Fried Rice with Tofu, 40
Cauliflower Mash with Fresh Thyme, 53
### celery
Corn and Sweet Potato Chowder, 24
Cabbage and White Bean Soup, 26
Tomato and Barley Soup with Thyme, 28
Quinoa and Kale Detox Soup, 30
Split Pea Soup with Fresh Herbs, 33
Vegan Bolognese with Whole-Grain Pasta, 41
Hearty Vegetable and Lentil Stew, 43
### cherries
Roasted Cherry and Almond Crisp, 62
### cherry tomatoes
Avocado and Spinach Egg White Omelette, 13
Zucchini Noodle Salad with Pesto, 26
Roasted Eggplant and Chickpea Salad Bowl, 42
### chia seeds
Berry Burst Chia Smoothie, 69
Chia-Infused Limeade, 74
### chickpeas
Quinoa-Stuffed Bell Peppers with Chickpeas, 35
Moroccan Chickpea and Vegetable Tagine, 38
Roasted Eggplant and Chickpea Salad Bowl, 42
Spicy Roasted Chickpeas, 50
Roasted Bell Pepper Hummus with Pita Wedges, 55
### chocolate chips
Chocolate-Covered Dates with Almond Butter Filling, 59
### coconut cream
Sugar-Free Lemon Coconut Bars, 60
coconut flour
Sugar-Free Lemon Coconut Bars, 60
### coconut milk
Sweet Potato and Lentil Curry, 35
Coconut Milk Rice Pudding with Mango, 57
Sesame and Coconut Mochi Bites, 63
### coconut water
Raspberry and Mint Lemonade Smoothie, 68
Tropical Pineapple and Spinach Smoothie Recipe, 69
Green Detox Smoothie with Cucumber and Kiwi, 69
### coconut yogurt
Raspberry and Mint Lemonade Smoothie, 68
Blueberry Oatmeal Breakfast Smoothie, 68
Berry Burst Chia Smoothie, 69
Matcha Green Tea and Banana Smoothie, 71
Pear Cardamom Shake, 75
Orange Sunshine Smoothie with Turmeric, 71
Spiced Pumpkin Pie Smoothie, 71
### cod
Baked Cod with Lemon and Herbs, 40
### coriander
Thai-Inspired Cabbage Slaw with Peanut Dressing, 25
### corn kernels
Corn and Sweet Potato Chowder, 24
### crackers
Smoky Eggplant Dip with Whole-Grain Crackers, 48
### cranberries
Broccoli and Cranberry Salad with Almonds, 24
### cranberry juice
Cranberry Ginger Fizz, 73
### cucumber
Summer Gazpacho with Fresh Herbs, 29
Mixed Greens with Orange and Pumpkin Seeds, 30

Roasted Eggplant and Chickpea Salad Bowl, 42
Avocado and Lime Guacamole with Veggie Sticks, 49
Green Detox Smoothie with Cucumber and Kiwi, 69
Minty Cucumber Cooler, 73

## D
### dates
Walnut and Date Breakfast Bars, 18

## E
### edamame
Edamame and Brown Rice Salad, 27
### egg whites
Banana and Walnut Whole-Grain Pancakes, 13
Avocado and Spinach Egg White Omelette, 13
### eggplant
Baked Eggplant Parmesan (Dairy-Free), 36
Roasted Eggplant and Chickpea Salad Bowl, 42
Smoky Eggplant Dip with Whole-Grain Crackers, 48
### enchilada sauce
Sweet Potato and Black Bean Enchiladas, 42

## G
### granola
Green Smoothie Bowl with Granola and Kiwi, 16
### grapefruit juice
Zesty Grapefruit and Ginger Spritz, 74
### green beans
Sesame Green Beans with Soy Glaze, 51

## H
### hibiscus flowers
Iced Hibiscus and Pomegranate Tea, 72

## K
### kale
Sweet Potato and Kale Breakfast Hash, 14
Quinoa Bowl with Sautéed Kale and Mushrooms, 22
Quinoa and Kale Detox Soup, 30
Butternut Squash and Kale Risotto, 43
Zesty Lemon Kale Smoothie, 70
### kiwi
Green Smoothie Bowl with Granola and Kiwi, 16
Green Detox Smoothie with Cucumber and Kiwi, 69

## L
### leek
Cauliflower and Leek Soup with Garlic Croutons, 32
### lemon
Zesty Lemon Kale Smoothie, 70
Blueberry Lemon Infused Water, 73
### lemon juice
Sugar-Free Lemon Coconut Bars, 60
Lemon and Blueberry Polenta Cake, 65
Raspberry and Mint Lemonade Smoothie, 68
### lentils
Lentil and Veggie Breakfast Scramble, 19
Lentil and Spinach Soup with a Hint of Lemon, 25
Sweet Potato and Lentil Curry, 35
Vegan Shepherd's Pie with Lentils and Sweet Potato, 37
Hearty Vegetable and Lentil Stew, 43
Hearty Lentil and Veggie Pâté, 52

### lime juice
Chia-Infused Limeade, 74

## M
### mango
Green Smoothie Bowl with Granola and Kiwi, 16
Coconut Milk Rice Pudding with Mango, 57
Mango and Passionfruit Sorbet, 60
### marinara sauce
Baked Eggplant Parmesan (Dairy-Free), 36
Baked Polenta Fries with Marinara Dip, 46
Baked Zucchini Sticks with Marinara Sauce, 47
### matcha powder
Matcha Green Tea and Banana Smoothie, 71
### medjool dates
Chocolate-Covered Dates with Almond Butter Filling, 59
Almond and Date Energy Bars, 61
### mint leaves
Minty Cucumber Cooler, 73
### mixed berries
Berry Burst Chia Smoothie, 69
Berry and Almond Butter Breakfast Wrap, 19
Beet and Berry Antioxidant Juice, 75
Mixed Greens with Orange and Pumpkin Seeds, 30
### mixed salad greens
Roasted Beet and Avocado Salad, 28
Roasted Eggplant and Chickpea Salad Bowl, 42
### mushrooms
Spinach and Mushroom Tofu Scramble, 16
Quinoa Bowl with Sautéed Kale and Mushrooms, 22
Roasted Garlic and Mushroom Soup, 31
Stuffed Portobello Mushrooms with Brown Rice, 38
Vegan Bolognese with Whole-Grain Pasta, 41
Mushroom and Barley Stuffed Cabbage Rolls, 44
Garlic and Herb Roasted Mushrooms, 47
Hearty Lentil and Veggie Pâté, 52

## O
### oat flour
Banana and Walnut Whole-Grain Pancakes, 13
### onion
Sweet Potato and Kale Breakfast Hash, 14
Corn and Sweet Potato Chowder, 24
Lentil and Spinach Soup with a Hint of Lemon, 25
Cabbage and White Bean Soup, 26
Broccoli and Pea Soup with Fresh Mint, 27
Tomato and Barley Soup with Thyme, 28
Quinoa and Kale Detox Soup, 30
Roasted Garlic and Mushroom Soup, 31
Split Pea Soup with Fresh Herbs, 33
Quinoa-Stuffed Bell Peppers with Chickpeas, 35
Sweet Potato and Lentil Curry, 35
Vegan Shepherd's Pie with Lentils and Sweet Potato, 37
Stuffed Portobello Mushrooms with Brown Rice, 38
Moroccan Chickpea and Vegetable Tagine, 38
Vegan Bolognese with Whole-Grain Pasta, 41
Butternut Squash and Kale Risotto, 43
Hearty Vegetable and Lentil Stew, 43
Mushroom and Barley Stuffed Cabbage Rolls, 44
Hearty Lentil and Veggie Pâté, 52
Spinach and Mushroom Tofu Scramble, 16
Lentil and Veggie Breakfast Scramble, 19
Veggie-Packed Savoury Oatmeal, 20

Broccoli and Cranberry Salad with Almonds, 24
Roasted Beet and Avocado Salad, 28
Summer Gazpacho with Fresh Herbs, 29
Mixed Greens with Orange and Pumpkin Seeds, 30
Warm Roasted Vegetable Salad with Balsamic Glaze, 31
Zesty Bean and Corn Salad, 32
Sweet Potato and Black Bean Enchiladas, 42
Sweet Corn Salad with Lime and Cilantro, 53
### orange
Mixed Greens with Orange and Pumpkin Seeds, 30
Carrot Ginger Immunity Smoothie, 70
### orange juice
Vegan Orange and Almond Cake, 64
Orange Sunshine Smoothie with Turmeric, 71

## P
### parsnips
Roasted Carrot and Parsnip Medley, 54
### passionfruit
Mango and Passionfruit Sorbet, 60
### pasta
Vegan Bolognese with Whole-Grain Pasta, 41
### peanut butter
Thai-Inspired Cabbage Slaw with Peanut Dressing, 25
Grilled Tofu Skewers with Peanut Sauce, 39
### pear
Oatmeal with Almond Milk, Cinnamon and Pears, 15
Pear Cardamom Shake, 75
Baked Cinnamon Pears with Walnuts, 57
### pearl (baby) onions
Balsamic Glazed Roasted Pearl (baby) Onions, 54
### pearl barley
Tomato and Barley Soup with Thyme, 28
Mushroom and Barley Stuffed Cabbage Rolls, 44
### peas
Broccoli and Pea Soup with Fresh Mint, 27
Cauliflower Fried Rice with Tofu, 40
### pineapple
Tropical Pineapple and Spinach Smoothie Recipe, 69
### pita breads
Roasted Bell Pepper Hummus with Pita Wedges, 55
### polenta
Baked Polenta Fries with Marinara Dip, 46
Lemon and Blueberry Polenta Cake, 65
### pomegranate
Quinoa Breakfast Bowl with Nuts and Pomegranate, 14
Vanilla Cashew Cream Pudding with Pomegranate, 64
### pomegranate juice
Iced Hibiscus and Pomegranate Tea, 72
### pumpkin puree
Pumpkin and Oat Breakfast Porridge, 21
Spiced Pumpkin Pie Smoothie, 71
### pumpkin seeds
Mixed Greens with Orange and Pumpkin Seeds, 30

## Q
### quinoa
Quinoa Breakfast Bowl with Nuts and Pomegranate, 14
Quinoa Bowl with Sautéed Kale and Mushrooms, 22
Quinoa and Kale Detox Soup, 30
Quinoa-Stuffed Bell Peppers with Chickpeas, 35
Roasted Vegetable Buddha Bowl with Tahini Dressing, 39
Apricot and Quinoa Cookies, 62

## R
### raisins
Carrot Cake Overnight Oats, 17
### raspberries
Almond Milk Panna Cotta with Raspberry Coulis, 66
Raspberry and Mint Lemonade Smoothie, 68
### rice
Butternut Squash and Kale Risotto, 43
Coconut Milk Rice Pudding with Mango, 57
### rice flour
Sesame and Coconut Mochi Bites, 63
### rolled oats
Oatmeal with Almond Milk, Cinnamon and Pears, 15
Zucchini and Red Pepper Breakfast Muffins, 15
Carrot Cake Overnight Oats, 17
Walnut and Date Breakfast Bars, 18
Veggie-Packed Savoury Oatmeal, 20
Pumpkin and Oat Breakfast Porridge, 21
Baked Oatmeal Cups with Blueberries and Walnuts, 22
Vegan Apple Crumble with Oats, 58
Vegan Blueberry Almond Tart, 61
Almond and Date Energy Bars, 61
Apricot and Quinoa Cookies, 62
Roasted Cherry and Almond Crisp, 62
Blueberry Oatmeal Breakfast Smoothie, 68

## S
### salmon
Baked Salmon with Garlic, Dill and Asparagus, 41
### sesame seeds
Sesame and Coconut Mochi Bites, 63
### sparkling water
Cranberry Ginger Fizz, 73
Zesty Grapefruit and Ginger Spritz, 74
### spinach
Avocado and Spinach Egg White Omelette, 13
Green Smoothie Bowl with Granola and Kiwi, 16
Spinach and Mushroom Tofu Scramble, 16
Veggie-Packed Breakfast Burrito, 17
Lentil and Veggie Breakfast Scramble, 19
Lentil and Spinach Soup with a Hint of Lemon, 25
Spinach and Strawberry Salad with Balsamic Glaze, 33
Tropical Pineapple and Spinach Smoothie Recipe, 69
Green Detox Smoothie with Cucumber and Kiwi, 69
### split peas
Split Pea Soup with Fresh Herbs, 33
### strawberries
Spinach and Strawberry Salad with Balsamic Glaze, 33
### sweet potato
Sweet Potato and Kale Breakfast Hash, 14
Sweet Potato Bowl with Almonds and Cinnamon, 18
Corn and Sweet Potato Chowder, 24
Sweet Potato and Lentil Curry, 35
Roasted Vegetable Buddha Bowl with Tahini Dressing, 39
Sweet Potato and Black Bean Enchiladas, 42
Sweet Potato Brownies with Cacao, 59
Vegan Shepherd's Pie with Lentils and Sweet Potato, 37
Baked Sweet Potato Wedges with Smoked Paprika, 46
### sweetcorn
Sweet Corn Salad with Lime and Cilantro, 53
Zesty Bean and Corn Salad, 32
Veggie-Packed Breakfast Burrito, 17
Sweet Corn and Zucchini Breakfast Fritters, 21

**T**

*tahini*
Roasted Eggplant and Chickpea Salad Bowl, 42

*tofu*
Spinach and Mushroom Tofu Scramble, 16
Teriyaki Tofu Stir-Fry with Brown Rice, 37
Grilled Tofu Skewers with Peanut Sauce, 39
Cauliflower Fried Rice with Tofu, 40
Crispy Baked Tofu Nuggets, 49

*tomatoes*
Tomato and Barley Soup with Thyme, 28
Vegan Bolognese with Whole-Grain Pasta, 41
Summer Gazpacho with Fresh Herbs, 29
Quinoa-Stuffed Bell Peppers with Chickpeas, 35
Sweet Potato and Lentil Curry, 35
Moroccan Chickpea and Vegetable Tagine, 38
Hearty Vegetable and Lentil Stew, 43

*tortillas*
Veggie-Packed Breakfast Burrito, 17
Berry and Almond Butter Breakfast Wrap, 19
Sweet Potato and Black Bean Enchiladas, 42

**V**

*vegetable broth*
Veggie-Packed Savoury Oatmeal, 20
Quinoa Bowl with Sautéed Kale and Mushrooms, 22
Corn and Sweet Potato Chowder, 24
Lentil and Spinach Soup with a Hint of Lemon, 25
Cabbage and White Bean Soup, 26
Broccoli and Pea Soup with Fresh Mint, 27
Tomato and Barley Soup with Thyme, 28
Quinoa and Kale Detox Soup, 30
Roasted Garlic and Mushroom Soup, 31
Cauliflower and Leek Soup with Garlic Croutons, 32
Split Pea Soup with Fresh Herbs, 33
Sweet Potato and Lentil Curry, 35
Vegan Shepherd's Pie with Lentils and Sweet Potato, 37
Moroccan Chickpea and Vegetable Tagine, 38

Butternut Squash and Kale Risotto, 43
Hearty Vegetable and Lentil Stew, 43
Herb-Infused Brown Rice Pilaf, 48

*vegetable juice*
Summer Gazpacho with Fresh Herbs, 29

**W**

*walnuts*
Walnut and Date Breakfast Bars, 18
Baked Oatmeal Cups with Blueberries and Walnuts, 22
Spinach and Strawberry Salad with Balsamic Glaze, 33
Baked Cinnamon Pears with Walnuts, 57
Vegan Apple Crumble with Oats, 58

*wheat flour*
Vegan Chocolate Banana Bread, 63
Vegan Orange and Almond Cake, 64
Banana and Walnut Whole-Grain Pancakes, 13
Zucchini and Red Pepper Breakfast Muffins, 15
Sweet Corn and Zucchini Breakfast Fritters, 21

*white beans*
Cabbage and White Bean Soup, 26

**Z**

*zucchini*
Zucchini and Red Pepper Breakfast Muffins, 15
Veggie-Packed Breakfast Burrito, 17
Lentil and Veggie Breakfast Scramble, 19
Veggie-Packed Savoury Oatmeal, 20
Sweet Corn and Zucchini Breakfast Fritters, 21
Warm Roasted Vegetable Salad with Balsamic Glaze, 31
Quinoa-Stuffed Bell Peppers with Chickpeas, 35
Moroccan Chickpea and Vegetable Tagine, 38
Grilled Tofu Skewers with Peanut Sauce, 39
Baked Salmon with Garlic, Dill and Asparagus, 41
Hearty Vegetable and Lentil Stew, 43
Zucchini Noodle Salad with Pesto, 26
Baked Zucchini Sticks with Marinara Sauce, 47

Printed in Great Britain
by Amazon